SAFEWAY
FRESH FOOD COOKBOOK

SAFEWAY

FRESH FOOD
COOKBOOK

Patrick Galvani

PREFACE

The formation of Safeway Food Stores Ltd. in the United Kingdom in 1962, represented the coming together of the latest American supermarket concepts, and an essentially traditional but still innovative form of British retailing. From small beginnings, the company has grown to the point that it now operates over 105 large supermarkets and superstores throughout England and Scotland. Safeway is committed to creative food marketing, coupled with service to the consumer, and in a period of changing shopping habits, it is company policy to ensure that the customer continues to be the most important person in a Safeway store.

This commitment to excellence in a wide variety of fresh foods has led to the publication of the *Safeway Fresh Food Cookbook*, which has been produced with the cooperation of Patrick Galvani who, with his wife Madeleine, owns the Laws Hotel at Turvey in North Bedfordshire. This small country house hotel has won many accolades from various restaurant guides, both in this country and North America. The Galvanis have been in the food trade for a combination of over 50 years: Patrick writes on food and drink for trade magazines, is a Chevalier du Tastevin and a member of the Chaine des Rôtisseurs, while Madeleine supervises the preparation and production of the food for the two restaurants at The Laws. Both have travelled widely and many of the recipes in this book reflect their visits abroad.

Forest pie (see page 51)

Published in 1984 for
Safeway Food Stores Ltd.
Beddow Way, Aylesford,
Maidstone, Kent

By Octopus Books Limited
59 Grosvenor Street
London W 1

ISBN 0 7064 2151 5

Printed in Hong Kong

Special Photography:
Bryce Attwell 16, 28, 72, 81; **Rex Bamber** 64; **Robert Golden** 84-85; **Melvin Grey** 52;
Norman Nicholls 69; **Paul Williams** 12-13, 20-21, 24, 29, 32, 37, 40-41, 44, 45, 48-49,
56-57, 60, 61, 68, 76-77, 88

CONTENTS

Introduction 12
Soups and starters 17
Fish and shellfish 25
Meat and poultry 33
Vegetable and vegetarian dishes 53
Uncooked dishes 65
Desserts and baking 73
Index 92

INTRODUCTION

The advantages of fresh food may seem obvious, but in these days of convenience foods, it's worth having another look at them. The flavour of fresh meat, fish, vegetables and fruit has more individuality and variety than manufactured foods.

When you buy fresh food you can check its appearance and quality for yourself and, because fresh food retains a considerable amount of its vitamins and minerals, you can plan meals which are nutritionally balanced as well as delicious.

Choosing and buying
Use your eyes when selecting fresh food: this is particularly important where you are not able to touch the produce although many supermarkets now allow you to pick your own fruit and vegetables from loose displays.

Meat should have a moist surface with clean fat; dry flesh is a sign that it has been exposed to the air for some time and may be stale. The best beef is home-produced – and expensive; it will not have been frozen or chilled for long periods, which toughens the meat although this does not matter so much with cheaper cuts which require long slow cooking anyway. Look for bright red lean

with a brownish tinge, and creamy fat. Lamb should be pinkish brown – the lighter the colour the younger the lamb – and its fat should be pale cream white. Veal should be a pale pearly pink with white fat. Avoid veal with bubbly tissue except for pies and stews. Pork should be rosy with white fat and elastic skin. Offal should always have a good strong colour and very moist texture.

Fresh poultry is often more expensive than frozen, but apart from having better flavour, it can also be better value, since a lot of water is lost from frozen birds during thawing. Look for clean, flexible skin without signs of bruising. Remember that undressed birds are sold at their original weight and take this into account when buying a large bird such as turkey, as it can make quite a difference to cooking times once head, legs and giblets are removed.

A keen nose and a sharp eye are essential when buying fish. Fish should always be as fresh as possible – and the fresher it is the less 'fishy' it will smell. Watch out for cloudy eyes and dull skin colouring – these are signs that the fish is old. Falling scales are not always a reliable guide as scales fall at different rates on different species. Shellfish must be absolutely fresh since, of all foods, these can cause the most unpleasant food poisoning. Molluscs such as mussels should be bought live; reject any that have open shells and equally reject any that refuse to open after cooking. Never buy crustaceans (crabs, lobsters etc.) when uncooked but dead.

Their shells should be red or pink when cooked. Prawns and shrimps are usually sold cooked as they perish quickly when raw.

Dairy produce such as eggs, cheese, yogurt and cream have to be chosen as carefully for freshness as fish or meat. Eggs carry a packing date and are graded by size: from 1 to 6 (or more than 70g to 45–50g). Common sense should guide you when buying other dairy produce. They should be stored in a chilled cabinet. Use the 'sell by' date as a guide for cream, yogurt and pre-packed cheeses – it is worth remembering that retailers err on the side of caution, so if the date has passed it does not necessarily mean that the product is inedible.

Some meat and fish are seasonal, in particular best lamb, game, salmon and some shellfish, so it is well to be informed about the periods of their availability. Watch also for seasonal bargains: fruit and vegetables are sold according to quality and are usually Class 1 in supermarkets and greengrocers; some open markets and farm shops sell Class 2 and Class 3, while luxury shops may sell superb Extra Class produce. Classes 2 and 3 are perfectly good in all respects except that they may not be uniform in size and appearance.

When buying green vegetables look for crisp leaves without too much discoloration or wasteful outer layers. Peas and broad beans should have firm shells; runner and French beans should be crisp not floppy. Avoid over-large runners as they tend to be stringy. Salad vegetables are obviously at their best between May and October; lettuce and tomatoes bought in winter are forced or imported, and expensive. Experiment with other types of salad, using readily available winter vegetables like carrots, celery and cabbage, or more unusual items such as celeriac and Chinese cabbage. Root vegetables should be bought when hard and dry to the touch; they do not have to be prewashed, but beware if they are caked in damp mud: scratch through to the skin and check for any hidden rot.

A few safe but rather dull varieties of basic fruits are now available throughout the year. But watch for seasonal changes; good English apples and pears from late August to Christmas; Spanish navel oranges and other citrus fruits from November to March; and, above all, the soft fruit season in early summer – fruits such as red and black currants are only available for a few weeks in the year. Avoid bruised fruit unless you are going to cook or eat it at once, since rot sets in quickly and can affect the whole purchase. Melon, peaches or nectarines bought a couple of days before required should be firmish, otherwise they should be soft enough to give slightly under light finger pressure. Colour is not always a good indicator of quality; some fruits are now cultivated to look luscious but taste of nothing!

Storage
Fresh foods need to be able to breathe, so remove any plastic or shrink-wrapping as soon as you get home. All meat and fish should be kept in the refrigerator until used, covered with greaseproof paper or a plate. Do not freeze fresh fish – it may have been frozen once already on board ship.

Keep root vegetables and hard greens like cabbage and cauliflower in a cool, dry place, preferably in a rack where air can circulate. Other vegetables are best kept in the salad crisper at the bottom of the refrigerator. Fruit becomes overripe quickly in a warm kitchen, so only stock the fruit bowl with what you need for a day or two. Keep apples, pears, bananas and citrus fruits in a cool, dry place, and other fruits in the refrigerator. Eggs and cheese are best kept in a cold larder and failing that, the refrigerator, but eggs must be allowed to return to room temperature before use, and soft cheeses like Brie or Camembert require at least two hours to 'breathe' before eating.

Do not try to keep fresh foods too long; they lose more than their freshness, for their vitamin content may deteriorate and their flavour certainly will. If you have a surplus, freeze what you do not need immediately or preserve it some other way. Jams and pickles may not be fresh, but they are still delicious and avoid heartbreaking waste.

Preparation and cooking

It is worth taking care with the preparation and cooking of fresh produce even for the simplest meal. Vegetables suffer most from thoughtless cooking, which can destroy flavour, texture and nutritional benefits. Wash vegetables quickly under cold running water; do not leave them to soak as many natural vitamins and minerals are water-soluble. A useful aid when washing leafy vegetables is a salad spinner, which uses centrifugal force to dry the leaves. Do not overcook green vegetables; five to seven minutes in already boiling water should be enough depending on quantity. The texture to aim for is *al dente* – tender but not soft. Much of the goodness in root vegetables lies just under the skin, so scrub rather than peel them. Potatoes are rich in Vitamin C, which is best preserved by baking them in their jackets. Otherwise peel the thinnest layer possible away and leave the skins on new potatoes.

Wipe meat and poultry clean before cooking. Beef and lamb joints, steaks and chops are all delicious served rare in the Continental manner. Pork and poultry, however should always be well done. Either way, when roasting do not stand the meat in fat; the most it needs is to be brushed over with oil or melted fat and if it is well covered in its own fat no extra fat of any kind is needed. Meat releases its own juices which can be used for basting. Experiment with low-fat cooking methods such as pressure-cooked pot roasts, grills, spit roasts, barbecues and chicken bricks.

All fish should be cleaned and tough scales scraped off before cooking. Fish is only too easy to overcook, so be very careful when poaching, grilling or frying. Try steaming (a fish kettle is a good investment for a large family), or baking fish in aluminium foil parcels to seal in the flavour.

The recipes which follow will give you plenty of scope for cooking with a wide variety of fresh foods, some familiar, some less so. So take a fresh look at food, and enjoy yourself.

Soups and Starters

Gardener's broth with sablées

Serves 4–6

45 g/1 ½ oz butter
340 g/12 oz leeks, sliced
225 g/8 oz brussels sprouts, shredded
225 g/8 oz green beans, sliced
825 ml/1 ½ pints stock
salt and freshly ground black pepper
1 tbsp lemon juice
1 tsp Worcestershire sauce
pinch of grated nutmeg
285 ml/½ pint milk or a mixture of milk
  and single cream

Sablées

170 g/6 oz plain flour
salt and freshly ground black pepper
cayenne pepper
120 g/4 oz butter, diced
85 g/3 oz grated cheese (preferably a
  mixture of Parmesan and Cheddar)
1 egg yolk
1 tbsp water
1 egg white or milk, to glaze
sesame seeds

1. First make the sablées. Sift the flour with a pinch of salt, pepper and cayenne into a bowl. Add the butter and rub it in until the mixture resembles fine breadcrumbs. Stir in the cheese. Add the egg yolk and water and mix to a firm dough. Shape into a 2.5 cm/1 inch roll, wrap in foil and chill until firm.
2. Preheat the oven to 190°C/375°F/Gas 5. Grease a baking sheet. Cut the dough into 5 mm/¼ inch thick slices and lay them on

Gardener's broth with sablées

the baking sheet. Brush with egg white or milk and sprinkle with sesame seeds. Bake for 10–12 minutes. Cool on a wire rack.
3. To make the soup, melt the butter in a large saucepan. Add the leeks and fry gently for 2–3 minutes, stirring frequently. Add the sprouts and beans together with the stock, salt, pepper, lemon juice, Worcestershire sauce and nutmeg and bring to the boil. Cover, reduce the heat and simmer for 25 minutes or until the vegetables are soft.
4. Cool the soup slightly then purée in a blender until smooth. Return to the rinsed pan. Add the milk or milk and cream mixture and boil for 2–3 minutes. Adjust the seasoning.
5. Serve with warmed cheese sablées.

Melon fruit cup

Serves 4–6

1 melon, halved and seeded
120 g/4 oz black grapes, halved and pips
  removed
120 g/4 oz white grapes, halved and pips
  removed
8–12 tbsp medium white wine

1. Scoop out balls from the melon flesh and arrange in coupe glasses or wide-necked wine glasses. Arrange the black and white grapes around the melon balls, in a decorative pattern.
2. Slowly pour the wine over the melon and grape mixture – there should be enough in each glass to come about a quarter way up the sides.

Note: Strawberries, raspberries or orange can be used instead of grapes.

Bisque creole

The okra used in this recipe gives the soup a
gummy consistency, and must be fresh.
Tinned pimientos have been used because
they give a better flavour to the soup and are
easier to cook and liquidize than fresh red
peppers.

Traditionally, Creole soups do not have
horseradish cream added, but it is included
here to give the soup an extra piquancy.

Serves 4–6

30 g/1 oz butter
2 tbsp chopped onion
*1 × 190 g/6½ oz tin pimientos, drained
and roughly chopped*
45 g/1½ oz flour
1 × 400 g/14 oz tin Italian tomatoes
*1.2 litres/2 pints chicken stock (made with
3 cubes)*
½ tsp cayenne pepper
salt and freshly ground black pepper
120 g/4 oz okra, trimmed and chopped
2 tsp horseradish cream
chopped parsley
cream

1. Melt the butter in a saucepan. Add the
onion and fry gently until just translucent.
Add the pimientos then the flour, stirring
until blended. Add the tomatoes and their
juice, the stock and cayenne and season to
taste. Finally, stir in the okra, and bring to
the boil. Cover, reduce the heat and simmer the soup for 25-30 minutes, or until
cooked and tender.
2. Cool the mixture slightly then purée in a
blender until smooth. Strain the soup back
into the rinsed pan, discarding the okra
seeds. Heat gently and, just before serving,
stir in the horseradish cream. Garnish with
a little chopped parsley and a swirl or two of
cream.

Apple and cabbage soup

Serves 6

1 tbsp oil
1 medium onion, chopped
1 clove garlic, chopped
*¼ white cabbage (about 450 g/1 lb),
trimmed and shredded*
*1.2 litres/2 pints chicken stock (made with
2 cubes)*
*450 g/1 lb cooking apples, peeled, cored
and quartered*
1 tbsp sugar
½ tsp chopped basil
freshly ground pepper
*150 ml/¼ pint whipping cream, stiffly
beaten (optional)*

1. In a large saucepan, sweat the onion and
garlic in the oil until soft. Stir in the cabbage and cook gently for 2–3 minutes until
it wilts. Pour over the stock and add the
remaining ingredients, except the cream.
Bring to the boil, cover the pan and reduce
the heat to low. Simmer for 20–30 minutes, or until the vegetables and apples are
cooked and soft.
2. Cool the mixture slightly then purée in a
blender or push through a sieve until
smooth. Return to the rinsed pan, adjust
the seasoning and reheat gently until hot
but not boiling.
3. Serve with dollops of whipped cream, if
liked, and accompanied by wholemeal or
pumpernickel bread.

Fresh vegetable soup

Serves 8–10

3 tbsp oil
1 large onion, chopped
3–4 carrots, diced
1 turnip or swede, chopped
2 leeks, chopped
½ fennel bulb, chopped
about 1 kg/2 lb (about 450 g/1 lb nett
weight) mixed vegetables, such as
cauliflower, broccoli, beans, peas,
courgettes, prepared for cooking
450 g/1 lb potatoes, peeled and chopped
about 1.75 litres/3 pints chicken stock
(made from 4 cubes)
freshly ground black pepper
1 tsp chopped mixed herbs

1. Heat the oil in a large saucepan. Add the onion and fry gently until soft. Stir in the carrots, turnip or swede, leeks, fennel, mixed vegetables and potatoes and fry for 3–4 minutes. Pour over the stock, season with the pepper and stir in the herbs.
2. Bring to the boil, cover the pan and simmer gently for 30–40 minutes or until all the vegetables are cooked through and the soup is good and thick.

Watercress soup

Serves 4–6

1 medium onion, chopped
1½ tbsp butter
2 packets watercress, trimmed and
chopped
225 g/8 oz cooked potatoes, diced
600 ml/1 pint milk
430 ml/¾ pint chicken stock
salt and freshly ground black pepper
85 ml/3 fl oz single cream

Chicken and sweetcorn soup

Serves 4

2 tbsp oil
1 large onion, finely chopped
¼ chicken (about 340 g/12 oz), skinned,
boned and chopped
1 carrot, thinly sliced
1 teaspoon chopped mixed herbs
salt and freshly ground black pepper
1.2 litres/2 pints good chicken stock
1 × 425 g/15 oz tin sweetcorn

1. Heat the oil in a large saucepan. Add the onion and fry gently until soft. Add the chicken with the carrot and cook, stirring frequently, until the meat has browned slightly. Stir in the herbs and season.
2. Stir about 285 ml/½ pint of stock into the pan and bring to the boil. Reduce the heat and simmer the mixture for 2–3 minutes. Stir in the sweetcorn, then pour in the remaining stock and bring to the boil. Reduce the heat to low and simmer, uncovered, for about 30 minutes or until the meat is tender and the soup has reduced to a fairly thick consistency.

1. In a saucepan, sweat the onion gently in the butter until just translucent. Stir in the watercress, potatoes, milk and stock and bring to the boil. Season to taste, reduce the heat and simmer for 5–8 minutes or until tender.
2. Cool the mixture slightly then purée in a blender until smooth. Return to the rinsed pan. Reheat gently until hot but not boiling, adding a little more milk if the soup needs thinning. Adjust the seasoning before serving. Garnish with a spoonful or two of cream in each bowl.

Fennel à la grecque

Serves 4

2 tbsp olive oil
2 heads of fennel, trimmed and sliced
  lengthways into quarters
juice of 1 lemon
1 tbsp chopped fresh marjoram or
  1 ½ tsp dried marjoram
1 ½ tsp ground coriander
salt and freshly ground black pepper
2 tbsp tomato purée
450 g/1 lb tomatoes, skinned, seeded and
  chopped
60 ml/2 fl oz white wine
1 tbsp chopped parsley

1. Heat the olive oil in a large saucepan. Put in the fennel, sprinkle with the lemon juice and fry until lightly coloured. Add the marjoram, coriander, and salt and pepper to taste and fry, stirring, for a further 2 minutes.

2. Stir in the tomato purée, tomatoes and wine. When bubbling, reduce the heat, half cover and simmer gently, stirring occasionally, for 30 minutes or until the fennel is tender. If the mixture becomes too dry during the cooking time, stir in a spoonful or two of water (or white wine, if preferred) to thin out.

3. Just before serving, adjust the seasoning and stir in the chopped parsley. Serve with crusty bread.

Deep fried mushrooms with chilli dip

Serves 4
1 egg, beaten
170 ml/6 fl oz milk
200 g/7 oz plain flour
225 g/8 oz matzo meal
24–32 medium button mushrooms,
*   trimmed*
oil for deep frying

Chilli dip
60 g/2 oz butter
1 small onion, chopped
1 green chilli, trimmed, seeded and finely
*   chopped*
1 clove garlic, crushed
pinch of chopped oregano
2 tsp tomato purée
pinch of chopped parsley
1 × 400 g/14 oz tin plum tomatoes,
*   blended to a purée with the juice*
120 ml/4 fl oz white wine

1. In a shallow bowl, combine the egg and milk together. Put the flour on one plate and the matzo meal on another. Dip the mushrooms, first in the flour, then in the egg and milk mixture and, finally, in the matzo meal, carefully shaking off any excess.
2. Fill a deep-frying pan about one-third full with oil and heat to about 180°C/350°F or, if you do not have a deep-frying thermometer, drop in a cube of stale bread. If it browns in 50 seconds the temperature will be about right. Fry the mushrooms, a few at a time, for about 45 seconds, or until they are browned and crisp. Remove, drain on absorbent paper and keep warm while you cook the remaining mushrooms and make the dip.
3. To make the dip, melt the butter in a small saucepan. Add the onion, chilli, garlic and oregano and fry gently until they are soft. Stir in the tomato purée and parsley. Add the blended tomatoes to the onion mixture with the wine. Simmer gently, uncovered, for 10 minutes or until thickened.
4. Serve the mushrooms immediately, with the chilli dip.

Deep fried mushrooms with chilli dip;
Fennel à la grecque

21

Chicken croquettes with pâté

These delicious chicken and pâté rissoles can be cooked either with matzo meal as here, or with fresh breadcrumbs.

Serves 4 (2 croquettes each)
225 g/8 oz cooked chicken, finely chopped
225 g/8 oz smooth liver pâté
salt and freshly ground black pepper
2 tsp chopped basil
120 g/4 oz medium matzo meal
85 g/3 oz plain flour, seasoned to taste with
  salt and freshly ground pepper
1 egg, beaten
85 ml/3 fl oz milk
oil for deep-frying

Mushroom sauce
1 small onion, finely chopped
85 g/3 oz button mushrooms, thinly sliced
15 g/½ oz butter
1 tsp plain flour
285 ml/½ pint chicken stock
1 tsp grated nutmeg
60 ml/2 fl oz single cream

1. Mix the chopped chicken, pâté, seasoning and basil together until thoroughly blended. Using floured hands, roll into 8 sausage shapes and chill in the refrigerator for at least 1 hour or until firm.
2. Next make the sauce. In a small saucepan, sweat the onion and mushrooms in the butter until soft. Add the flour and stir for a few seconds, then gradually stir in the chicken stock. Cook for 2–3 minutes until the sauce thickens, then stir in the nutmeg and cream. Remove from the heat and keep warm while you prepare the rissoles.
3. In a shallow bowl, combine the egg and milk together. Put the matzo meal in one bowl and the seasoned flour in another. Dip

the rissoles, first in the flour, shaking off any excess, then in the egg and milk mixture and, finally, in the matzo meal, shaking off any excess.
4. Fill a deep-frying pan about one-third full with oil and heat to about 180°C/350°F or, if you do not have a deep-frying thermometer, drop in a cube of stale bread. If it browns in 50 seconds the temperature will be about right. Fry the rissoles, a few at a time, for about 3–5 minutes or until they are browned and crisp. Remove, drain on absorbent paper and keep warm while you cook the remaining rissoles.
5. Serve, with the mushroom sauce.

Easy chicken liver pâté

Serves 6
15 g/½ oz lard
450 g/1 lb chicken livers, trimmed and
  chopped
170 g/6 oz fat pork
150 g/5 oz onions, sliced
2 tsp chopped mixed herbs
1 clove garlic, crushed
salt and freshly ground black pepper
2 tbsp medium sherry
2 tbsp whipping cream
30–60 g/1–2 oz butter

1. Melt the lard in a saucepan and add all the remaining ingredients except the sherry, cream and butter. Cook, stirring frequently, until the livers have lost their pinkness. Blend to a purée.
2. Transfer the mixture to a bowl and beat in the sherry and cream until blended. Spoon into small individual ramekin dishes or one large pâté dish.
3. Melt enough butter to form a coating over the chosen dishes or dish. Chill in the refrigerator until needed.

Prawn and cheese pancakes

Serves 4

60 g/2 oz butter
30 g/1 oz plain flour
430 ml/¾ pint milk
170 g/6 oz Cheddar cheese, grated
225 g/8 oz frozen peeled prawns,
  defrosted and drained
salt and freshly ground black pepper
parsley

Pancake batter

75 g/2½ oz plain flour
salt
1 egg
150 ml/¼ pint milk
3 tbsp oil or melted butter

1. First make the pancake batter. Sift the flour with a pinch of salt into a bowl. Make a well in the centre and break in the egg. Using a wire whisk or wooden spoon, beat the egg then gradually add the milk beating all the while and incorporating the flour slowly. Add 1 tbsp of the oil or butter and beat until the batter is smooth. Set aside.
2. Make a cheese sauce by melting the butter in a saucepan. Remove from the heat and stir in the flour to make a smooth paste. Slowly add the milk, stirring all the time. Return to the heat and simmer gently, stirring constantly, until the sauce is thick and smooth. Finally, stir in 100 g/4 oz of the grated cheese until it melts. Remove the pan from the heat. Preheat the oven to 200°C/400°F/Gas 6.
3. To make the pancakes, lightly grease a small, heavy frying pan (about 20 cm/8 inches in diameter) with a little of the remaining oil or butter, and heat it until very hot. Then pour a small ladleful of batter into the centre, tipping and rotating the pan so that the batter spreads evenly over the bottom. Cook quickly until the underside has browned, then flip over with a spatula and cook the second side until it, too, has browned. Cook the remaining batter in this way, stacking the pancakes on a plate, each separated by greaseproof paper to prevent them sticking together.
4. Put a quarter of the prawns on each of 4 pancakes, tuck in the sides and roll up envelope style so that the filling is completely enclosed. Arrange the pancakes in an ovenproof dish.
5. Pour over the cheese sauce, then sprinkle over the remaining grated cheese and season to taste. Bake in the oven for about 10–15 minutes or until the cheese has melted and is beginning to brown. Serve garnished with parsley.

Smoked mackerel pâté

Serves 8

450 g/1 lb smoked mackerel, skin and
  bones removed
120 g/4 oz butter
225 ml/8 fl oz whipping cream, beaten
2 tsp lemon juice
salt and freshly ground pepper
pinch of cayenne

1. Mash the mackerel flesh in a large bowl. Melt half the butter and add to the mackerel, then purée to a smooth paste in a blender. Scrape out the paste into the bowl.
2. Beat in the cream, lemon juice, seasoning to taste and the cayenne until well mixed. Spoon into 8 individual ramekin dishes.
3. Melt the remaining butter and pour a little over each of the ramekins, to cover the pâté. Chill in the refrigerator until needed.

FISH AND SHELLFISH

Salmon with cold cucumber sauce

Serves 4

4 × 170 g/6 oz salmon steaks
1 bay leaf
6 peppercorns
1 tbsp chopped onion

Cucumber Sauce

½ cucumber, peeled, seeded and finely
    chopped
285 ml/½ pint natural yogurt
2 tsp chopped mint
salt and freshly ground pepper
4 mint sprigs
4 lemon wedges

1. First make the sauce. Drain the cucumber and put it into a bowl. Mix in the yogurt, mint and salt and pepper to taste. Cover and chill.
2. Put the salmon steaks into a large frying pan. Cover with water and add the bay leaf, peppercorns and onion. Cover the pan and simmer for 10 minutes or until the salmon is cooked through.
3. Transfer the salmon steaks to a board and, if you wish, remove the skin and centre bone with a sharp knife.
4. Serve garnished with the mint sprigs and lemon wedges. Serve the sauce separately, in a sauceboat, or spooned on to the side of the plate. A crisp, dry white wine is best with salmon – Chablis is traditional.

Salmon with cold cucumber sauce

Sardines with tomato and basil sauce

Serves 4

4 tbsp plus a little extra olive oil
16 fresh sardines, cleaned
4 cloves garlic
4 tsp dried basil
½ tsp salt
freshly ground black pepper
butter for frying
2 tbsp finely chopped onion
120 ml/4 fl oz dry white wine
8–10 tomatoes, skinned, seeded and
    chopped
1 tbsp chopped parsley

1. Preheat the oven to 190°C/375°F/Gas 5. Oil a large casserole dish and put in the sardines in one or two layers.
2. Mash the garlic cloves, the 4 tablespoonfuls of olive oil, the basil, salt and black pepper in a mortar.
3. Melt the butter in a saucepan. Add the onion and fry over high heat, stirring constantly, for ½–1 minute or until brown. Add the wine and cook over high heat, stirring constantly, until nearly all the wine has evaporated. Stir in the basil and garlic mixture. Add the tomatoes and continue cooking until they are reduced to a gungy mush. Remove from the heat and pour over the sardines.
4. Put the casserole into the oven and bake for 20 minutes or until the sardines are cooked.
5. Garnish with the chopped parsley before serving. Try a medium-dry white wine or, for a change, a soft medium pink, with this dish.

Cod florentine

Serves 4

450 g/1 lb frozen leaf spinach
4 × 170–225 g/6–8 oz cod steaks
2 bay leaves
6 peppercorns
butter
60 g/2 oz Cheddar cheese, grated

Cheese sauce

45 g/1 ½ oz butter
45 g/1 ½ oz flour
600 ml/1 pint milk
85 g/3 oz Cheddar cheese, grated
salt
pinch of cayenne pepper

1. Cook the spinach according to the instructions on the packet. Drain well by pressing between two saucers.
2. Put the cod steaks into a large frying pan. Cover with water and add the bay leaves and peppercorns. Cover and simmer for 7–8 minutes or until the fish is cooked through.
3. Transfer the cod steaks to a board and, using a sharp knife, remove the skin and bone. Set aside while you make the sauce.
4. To make the sauce, melt the butter in a saucepan. Remove from the heat and stir in the flour to make a smooth paste. Slowly add the milk, stirring. Return to the heat and, stirring constantly, slowly bring the sauce to the boil. Simmer for 1–2 minutes then add the cheese, salt to taste and the cayenne, stirring until the sauce is smooth.
5. Preheat the oven to 180°C/350°F/Gas 4. Butter an ovenproof dish. Lay the spinach evenly on the bottom and arrange the cod steaks over the spinach. Cover with the cheese sauce. Sprinkle with the grated Cheddar and cook in the oven for 20–25 minutes or until browned on top.
6. Serve at once with a medium-dry or medium-sweet white wine.

Madeleine's fish pie

Serves 4–6

450 g/1 lb haddock fillets, cooked and
skinned
6 hard-boiled eggs
salt and freshly ground pepper
1 kg/2 lb cooked potatoes,
mashed
60 g/2 oz Cheddar cheese, grated

Cheese sauce

45 g/1 ½ oz butter
45 g/1 ½ oz flour
600 ml/1 pint milk
85 g/3 oz Cheddar cheese, grated
salt and freshly ground black
pepper

1. Flake the fish with the eggs and place in an ovenproof casserole. Season to taste with salt and pepper. Preheat the oven to 180°C/350°F/Gas 4.
2. To make the cheese sauce, melt the butter in a saucepan. Remove from the heat and stir in the flour to make a smooth paste. Slowly add the milk, stirring all the time. Return to the heat and simmer gently, stirring constantly, until the sauce thickens. Stir in the cheese until it melts. Season to taste.
3. Pour the sauce over the fish and cover with the mashed potato. Sprinkle over the grated Cheddar. Bake in the oven for 30 minutes or until the top is crispy and golden.
4. Serve at once. Accompany with chilled lager or a medium-sweet or medium-dry white wine.

Rainbow trout in oatmeal

Serves 4

*4 trout, cleaned and gutted, heads and tails
 removed*
salt and freshly ground black pepper
85–120 g/3–4 oz oatmeal
butter for frying

1. Open out the fish and pull out the main
part of the backbone, starting at the head
end. Tease out the small bones at the edges.
2. Wash thoroughly, pat dry and sprinkle
with salt, inside and out, then coat with
oatmeal. Season with black pepper.
3. Melt the butter in a frying pan large
enough to take the trout in one layer.
Arrange the fish in the pan, skin side down,
and cook for 5–6 minutes, turning from
time to time, to brown evenly and cook
through. Add more fat during cooking if
necessary.
4. Serve at once. A crisp dry white wine is
best with trout.

Lemon sole with mustard sauce

Serves 4

fillets of 2 lemon sole

Mustard Sauce

60 g/2 oz butter
½ medium onion, finely sliced
1 tbsp lemon juice
85 ml/3 fl oz white wine
1 tbsp Dijon mustard
150 ml/¼ pint whipping cream

Scampi Galvani

The best scampi to use in this recipe is the
plain frozen jumbo type (usually sold in
450 g/1 lb packs) – don't use breaded
scampi.

Serves 4–6

60 g/2 oz butter
450 g/1 lb frozen scampi, thawed
450 g/1 lb peeled prawns, thawed if frozen
120 g/4 oz sweetcorn kernels
2 tbsp brandy
1 tbsp tomato purée
175 ml/6 fl oz whipping cream

1. Melt the butter in a frying pan. Add the
shellfish and simmer, stirring occasionally,
for 5 minutes.
2. Add the sweetcorn, brandy and tomato
purée and simmer for a further 3–4 minutes. Stir in the cream and allow it to heat
through and thicken.
3. Serve over rice. Crisp dry white wine or,
for a special treat, sparkling white wine,
would complement scampi well.

1. First make the sauce. Melt the butter in a
frying pan large enough to take the fillets in
one layer. Add the onion and fry gently until
translucent. Stir in the lemon juice and
wine and bring to the boil. Stir in the
mustard, then the cream and simmer for
1–2 minutes until the sauce is smooth and
well blended.
2. Carefully arrange the fillets in the sauce
and simmer for 5 minutes on each side or
until cooked through. Using a slotted
spoon, transfer the fillets to a warm serving
dish.
3. Spoon the sauce over the fillets and serve
at once. A medium dry white wine would be
excellent with sole.

Moules à la marinière

Moules à la marinière

Serves 4

about 3 litres/5 pints fresh mussels
60 g/2 oz butter
1 onion, finely chopped
340 ml/12 fl oz dry or medium white wine
2 tbsp lemon juice
1 bouquet garni
salt and freshly ground black pepper
1 tbsp flour
2 tbsp chopped fresh parsley
4 tbsp cream (optional)

1. Scrub the mussels in several changes of water to remove the beards, mud, sand and barnacles. The mussels must be tightly closed. If they do not close when tapped sharply, discard them.
2. Melt half the butter in a large saucepan. Add the onion and fry gently for a few minutes until soft. Add the wine, 150 ml/¼ pint water, lemon juice, bouquet garni and plenty of salt and pepper and bring to the boil. Cover and simmer for 4–5 minutes.
3. Uncover the pan and add the mussels. Cover and simmer for 5 minutes, shaking the pan frequently, until all the mussels have opened. Discard any that remain closed, and the bouquet garni.
4. Remove the pan from the heat and strain the liquor into a small pan. Discard the empty half shell from each mussel.
5. Gently heat the liquor. Mash the remaining butter with the flour to make beurre manié. Whisk it a little at a time into the liquor. Increase the heat and boil for 2 minutes. Stir in half the parsley and all of the cream, if you are using it. Pour the sauce over the mussels.
6. Reheat thoroughly then ladle the mussels and the sauce into 4 heated soup bowls and sprinkle with chopped parsley.
7. Serve with plenty of French bread and, to drink, a dry white wine.

Seafood risotto

Serves 4–6

120 g/4 oz plus 30 g/1 oz butter
1 small onion, chopped
2 cloves garlic, chopped
3 tomatoes, skinned, seeded and chopped
225 g/8 oz peeled prawns
225 g/8 oz frozen crab claws, thawed, or
squid, white part only, cut into pieces
225 g/8 oz monkfish, boned and cut into
pieces
2 tbsp plus extra grated Parmesan
450 g/1 lb Italian rice
285 ml/½ pint dry white wine
825 ml/1 ½ pints hot chicken stock
120 g/4 oz button mushrooms, sliced
salt and freshly ground black pepper
whole prawns
lemon slices

Seafood risotto

1. Melt the 120 g/4 oz butter in a large frying pan. Add the onion and garlic and fry until soft. Add the tomatoes, prawns, crab or squid, monkfish and 2 tbsp Parmesan and fry, stirring occasionally, for 3 minutes.
2. Stir in the rice. Pour in the wine slowly, stirring all the time. Bring to the boil then reduce to a simmer. Keep the pan uncovered and, when the rice has taken up all the wine, add a cup of stock. Continue simmering and when the stock has been taken up add another cup. Continue in this way until the rice is cooked but *al dente* or still a little chewy. This should take about 15–20 minutes and the rice should look moist. Do not worry if all the stock is not used up or if you need more liquid – just add a spoonful or two of water. Add the mushrooms and seasoning 5 minutes before the end of cooking time.
3. To serve, stir in the remaining butter and sprinkle some Parmesan over the top. Garnish with whole prawns and lemon slices.

Vol au vents of scallops and leeks

Serves 4

2 large leeks
8 fresh scallops, removed from their shells,
*   or 450 g/1 lb frozen scallops*
15 g/½ oz butter
60 ml/2 fl oz cream
1 tsp grated nutmeg
salt and freshly ground black pepper
4 large frozen vol-au-vent cases, or
*   8 medium cases*
cayenne pepper

1. Trim off most of the green part of the leeks, then clean thoroughly under cold running water. Pat dry with paper towels then slice finely into rings. If using fresh scallops, make sure that they are washed and cleaned and keep only the white muscle and pink coral.

2. Melt the butter in a frying pan. Add the leeks and sauté with the cream, nutmeg and salt and pepper to taste for 2–3 minutes. Add the scallops and cook with the leeks for 2–3 minutes on each side.

3. Using a slotted spoon, transfer the scallops and leeks to a warmed dish. Keep hot while you reduce the sauce to a rich thickness, adding a little more cream if necessary.

4. Heat up the vol au vents in the oven according to packet instructions.

5. Return the scallops and leeks to the rich sauce and baste well. Heat through for a minute or so then, when the vol au vents are ready, spoon the mixture into the middle, allowing the sauce to run down the sides. Sprinkle with a little cayenne pepper to colour.

6. Serve with fresh green beans and a colourful vegetable such as carrots, as a rich lunch or supper dish. One medium vol au vent, served on its own, makes an excellent starter. An elegant, crisp dry white wine, such as Muscadet, would complement this dish well.

Crab-burgers

This is an adaptation of the traditional American crabcake. Do not be tempted to use frozen crab for this recipe – it is too wet to handle properly.

Serves 4

450–500 g/16–18 oz fresh crabmeat,
*   mixed white and dark meat*
1 tbsp lemon juice
1 tbsp Worcestershire sauce
1 tsp mustard powder
1 egg, beaten
1 tbsp melted butter
1 tbsp flour plus extra for coating
1 tbsp thick mayonnaise
60 g/2 oz fresh breadcrumbs
1 tbsp chopped parsley
salt and freshly ground black pepper
butter for frying

1. Put all the ingredients, except the coating flour and the butter needed for frying, into a bowl and beat until thoroughly blended.

2. Using your hands, shape the mixture into 8 small burgers or cakes. Coat gently in flour, shaking off any excess. Chill in the refrigerator for 1 hour.

3. Melt some butter in a large frying pan. Add the burgers and cook for about 5–8 minutes, turning occasionally, or until heated through and golden brown.

4. Serve with petits pois and rice and, to drink, a crisp dry or medium white wine or dry cider.

Calamares a la plancha

Calamares are squid, a very under-rated fish in this country. A la plancha, in Spain where this recipe originates, simply means cooked on the grill – one of the best ways to cook this delicious fish.

Serves 4
8 squid
2 cloves garlic
1 tbsp chopped parsley
2 ½ tbsp olive oil
2 tsp paprika
1 tsp lemon juice
salt and freshly ground pepper

1. Rinse the squid thoroughly. Discard the quill. Pull the head away from the body. Sever the tentacles and reserve them. Discard the rest of the head. Peel the skin away from the body pouch. Remove and skin the side fins.
2. Pat the flesh dry with kitchen paper towels, then cut into even-sized slices.
3. Put a heavy iron griddle or good quality non-stick pan over high heat. When the griddle is hot, add the squid. Cook, turning frequently, for 6–8 minutes.
4. Meanwhile, mash the garlic cloves and parsley together in a mortar with the olive oil, paprika, lemon juice and seasoning to taste. Pour the mixture carefully over the squid, turning the fish slowly as you do, so that it is well coated.
5. Serve the squid hot, with lots of salad and crunchy bread. To drink, try a medium Spanish white wine.

Gratin of monkfish

Serves 4
750–800 g/1 ½ – 1 ¾ lb monkfish
120 g/4 oz butter
60 g/2 oz plain flour
1 tsp English mustard
salt and freshly ground black
  pepper
430 ml/¾ pint milk
60 g/2 oz Cheddar cheese, grated
60 g/2 oz fresh breadcrumbs
1 tbsp grated Parmesan cheese

1. Wash and bone the fish. Slice into finger-size pieces.
2. Make a cheese sauce, by melting half the butter in a saucepan. Remove from the heat and stir in the flour to make a smooth paste. Stir in the mustard and seasoning to taste. Slowly add the milk, stirring all the time. Return to the heat and simmer gently, stirring constantly, until the sauce thickens. Stir in the cheese until it melts. Remove from the heat.
3. Melt the remaining butter in a large frying pan. Add the fish and cook for 3–5 minutes, turning occasionally, until browned and cooked through. Transfer the fish to a flameproof casserole dish and pour over the sauce. Sprinkle over the breadcrumbs and grated Parmesan and brown under a hot grill for a few minutes until the topping bubbles.
4. Serve at once, straight from the dish, with a selection of crisp fresh vegetables. Serve with chilled lager or, if serving wine, try a medium-sweet white wine.

MEAT AND POULTRY

Braised beef Nivernaise

Serves 4

1 kg/2 lb lean braising steak, cubed
flour for coating
12 shallots, peeled and whole or
   3 medium onions, quartered
6 carrots, thinly sliced
lard for frying
430 ml/¾ pint beef stock
1 bouquet garni

Marinade

340 ml/12 fl oz medium dry white wine
2 carrots, thinly sliced
1 onion, sliced
1 tbsp chopped parsley
1 tsp chopped thyme
2 bay leaves
1–2 cloves garlic, crushed
6 juniper berries, lightly crushed (optional)

1. To make the marinade, combine all the ingredients in a large shallow bowl. Add the beef cubes, turning them over to coat. Cover and set aside at room temperature for at least 2 hours, or overnight in the refrigerator.
2. Using a slotted spoon, remove the meat from the marinade and pat dry with absorbent paper towels. Reserve the marinade. Roll the cubes in flour to coat then transfer to a large flameproof casserole.
3. Pour the marinade into a saucepan and bring to the boil. Reduce the heat and simmer gently for about 15 minutes, then strain into a bowl or jug. Preheat the oven to 180°C/350°F/Gas 4.

ABOVE: Beef olives (see page 35); BELOW: Braised beef nivernaise

4. Meanwhile, fry the shallots or onions and carrots gently in the lard for about 5 minutes. Transfer to the casserole and arrange them over the meat. Pour over the reduced marinade and the stock. Finally, place the bouquet garni in the casserole. Bring to the boil on the top of the stove then simmer for 5 minutes.
5. Cover the casserole and put it into the oven for 3–4 hours or until the meat is tender. Remove the bouquet garni.
6. Serve straight from the casserole. A light dry or full soft red wine makes an excellent accompaniment.

Granny's hamburgers

Serves 6 (about 24 meatballs)

1 kg/2 lb chuck steak, minced twice
1 egg
3 tbsp grated onion
1 tsp salt
freshly ground black pepper
flour for coating
lard for frying

1. Mix together all the ingredients, except the flour and lard, in a bowl.
2. Form the mixture into small balls, about the size of a table tennis ball, and roll, one at a time, in the flour to coat, shaking off any excess. Set aside to 'rest' on a board for 10–15 minutes.
3. Melt the lard in a large frying pan. Add the balls, a few at a time, and cook for about 5 minutes, turning occasionally, or until cooked to your liking.
4. Serve hot with barbecue or tomato sauce, or cold with a relish or mustard. To drink, try lager or a light dry red wine.

Goulash Galvani

Serves 4–6

45 g/1 ½ oz lard
1.5 kg/3 lb best chuck steak, trimmed of fat
*   and cubed*
2 large onions, roughly chopped
1 tbsp paprika
2–3 cloves garlic, crushed
1 tbsp plain flour
1 tsp cornflour
pinch of dried chillis
pinch of caraway seeds
1 × 60 g/2 oz tin tomato purée
1 × 400 g/14 oz tin plum tomatoes
salt and freshly ground black pepper
430 ml/¾ pint chicken stock
120 ml/4 fl oz sour cream

1. Melt two-thirds of the lard in a large deep frying pan. Add the meat and fry, turning occasionally, until evenly browned. Remove the meat *and* the juices from the pan and set aside in a bowl.

2. Add the remaining lard to the pan and fry the onions until translucent. Add more lard if necessary. Now return the meat juices to the pan (but not the meat) and simmer slowly for a few minutes until the onions are soft and brownish.

3. Add to the pan each of the following, stirring in one by one – do it without rushing: the paprika, garlic, flour (the mixture should now start to get 'gungy'), cornflour, chillis and caraway seeds, and the tomato purée. The mixture should now be 'gungy' – take great care not to let it burn. Now stir in the tomatoes and their juice, salt and pepper to taste and the stock and simmer for 2–3 minutes, stirring from time to time.

4. Preheat the oven to 170°C/325°F/Gas 3. Put the meat into the pan, stir and simmer for a few more minutes.

5. Transfer the goulash to a heavy-based casserole, cover and put it into the oven. Cook for about 2½ hours or until the meat is very tender.

6. A few minutes before the end of the cooking time remove the casserole from the oven and gently stir in the sour cream. Return the casserole to the oven to finish cooking.

7. Adjust the seasoning if necessary. Serve with buttered noodles or tagliatelle, and with a hearty full soft red wine.

Grilled sirloin steaks with green herbs

Serves 4

4 tbsp chopped parsley
2 tbsp chopped chervil
120 ml/4 fl oz double cream
30 g/1 oz butter
salt and freshly ground black
*   pepper*
4 sirloin steaks, trimmed, each about
*   2.5 cm/1 inch thick*

1. Mix the herbs with the cream and set aside for 30 minutes.

2. Melt the butter in a saucepan. Stir in the herb mixture and simmer gently until the mixture has reduced and thickened. Set aside.

3. Meanwhile season the steaks and cook them under a preheated hot grill for 3–5 minutes for rare, 6–7 minutes for medium and 8–9 minutes for well done, turning them once. Transfer to a warmed serving dish.

4. Spoon over the sauce and serve at once. A dry French red wine such as claret is the traditional accompaniment to steak. Or try a good Spanish rioja wine or Italian Chianti, for a change of taste.

Beef olives

Serves 6

450 g/1 lb finely minced beef
85 g/3 oz mushrooms, chopped
2 tsp mustard powder
1 medium onion, finely chopped
1 egg
1 tbsp chopped parsley
6 × 85 g/3 oz slices of topside, cut very thin
30 g/1 oz cooking fat

Sauce

1 medium onion, finely chopped
85 g/3 oz mushrooms, chopped
30 g/1 oz cooking fat
1 tbsp tomato purée
2 tbsp flour
600 ml/1 pint beef stock (made with cube)
1 tbsp chopped parsley

1. Mix together all the ingredients, except the beef, fat and sauce ingredients. Lay the beef slices on a board.
2. Form the stuffing mixture into 6 sausage shapes and lay one in the middle of each beef slice. Roll up, tucking in the sides. Secure with cocktail sticks or string.
3. Melt the cooking fat in a large frying pan. Add the beef olives and cook briskly, turning occasionally, until browned. Transfer to an ovenproof casserole. Preheat the oven to 190°C/375°F/Gas 5.
4. To make the sauce, fry the onion and mushrooms in the fat remaining in the pan for 4–5 minutes, stirring and adding more fat as necessary. Add the tomato purée and flour and mix well. Slowly stir in the stock. Simmer for 5 minutes then add parsley and salt and pepper to taste.
5. Pour the sauce over the beef olives. Cover the dish and cook in the oven for 1½ hours or until the beef is tender. Remove the cocktail sticks or string before serving.

Beef vindaloo

Serves 4–6

4 tbsp sunflower oil
1 large onion, finely chopped
4 cloves garlic, finely chopped
4 carrots, cut into oval slices
1 tbsp vindaloo curry paste
1.5 kg/3 lb lean braising steak, cubed
4 slices root ginger, peeled and chopped
6 small potatoes, halved
seeds of 6 green cardamom pods
1 tsp turmeric
1 tsp salt
½ tsp ground cumin
1 tsp garam masala
1 tsp ground coriander
600 ml/1 pint chicken stock
3 bay leaves
3 tomatoes, skinned and quartered
1 cinnamon stick

1. Heat the oil in a large saucepan. Add the garlic and fry over high heat for 1 minute, stirring. Add the carrots and fry for 5 minutes. Reduce the heat to medium and add the curry paste. Stir well for 30 seconds.
2. Add the beef and fry, stirring all the time, for 1 minute. Stir in the ginger and then the potatoes. Add the cardamom, turmeric, salt, cumin, garam masala and coriander. Stir then slowly add the stock. Bring to the boil, reduce to a simmer and add the bay leaves, tomatoes and cinnamon.
3. Cover the pan and simmer for 45 minutes. Uncover and simmer for a further 45 minutes or until the beef is tender and the sauce has thickened. If the sauce becomes too thick stir in a little water. Remove bay leaves and cinnamon before serving.
4. Serve with a rice, poppadums and chutney. Lager is usually served with curries rather than wine – but if wine is preferred, then stick to a light dry white.

Roast leg of lamb with herb coating

Serves 4

6 juniper berries
4 cloves garlic
1 tsp dried rosemary
1 tsp dried savory leaves
1 tsp dried marjoram
salt and freshly ground black pepper
2 tbsp sunflower oil
1 × 2 kg/4 lb leg of lamb, boned and rolled
4 tbsp chopped parsley
85 g/3 oz fresh breadcrumbs
30 g/1 oz butter
1 tbsp red wine vinegar

1. Crush the juniper berries in a mortar. Add the garlic and crush again. Add the herbs, seasoning and oil and continue to pound until the mixture forms a paste.
2. Spread the mixture all over the lamb then set aside at room temperature for at least 2–3 hours.
3. Preheat the oven to 220°C/425°F/Gas 7. When ready to cook, transfer the lamb to a roasting tin and roast in the oven for about 1½ hours if you like your lamb pink, a little longer if you prefer it well done.
4. Meanwhile, make a coating by mixing together the parsley and breadcrumbs. Melt the butter and add to the mixture with the vinegar to make a paste.
5. Halfway through cooking, remove the lamb from the oven and spoon out 2 tablespoonfuls of the cooking juices and mix into the parsley paste. Coat the top of the lamb with this mixture. Return the lamb to the oven and finish cooking.
6. Serve at once. A light dry red wine such as claret or a Chianti classico wine would go well with roast lamb.

Beef with pasta

Serves 4

4 tbsp olive oil
2 tsp garlic purée
1 tsp chopped rosemary
800 g/1 ¾ lb stewing beef or blade steak, cubed
½ tsp mixed spice
salt and freshly ground black pepper
150 ml/¼ pint red wine
1 tbsp chopped parsley
1 × 60 g/2 oz tin tomato purée
chopped oregano, basil and sage
340 g/12 oz pasta, such as penne, spaghetti or tagliatelle
knob of butter

1. Heat the oil in a saucepan. Add the garlic and rosemary and fry gently until the garlic is translucent. Stir in the meat, mixed spice and salt and pepper to taste, and fry until the meat is evenly browned.
2. Stir in the wine, parsley, tomato purée and a pinch each of oregano, basil and sage. Cover and simmer for about 2 hours, stirring occasionally, or until the meat is tender.
3. Just before the end of cooking time, cook the pasta according to the packet instructions. Drain well and transfer to a warmed serving bowl. Stir in the butter and season to taste.
4. Spoon over the meat sauce and serve at once. A light dry red Italian wine such as Chianti or Bardolino would be an excellent accompaniment.

Roast leg of lamb with herb coating; Shredded leeks (see page 62)

Navarin printanier

Serves 6

1.25–1.5 kg/2½–3 lb shoulder of lamb,
 trimmed of fat and cubed
salt and freshly ground black pepper
1 tsp sugar
30 g/1 oz butter
1 large onion, chopped
4 carrots, quartered
3 cloves garlic, crushed
2 tbsp flour
150 ml/¼ pint dry white wine
1 tbsp tomato purée
600 ml/1 pint beef stock
2 bouquets garnis
2 tbsp oil
12 shallots, peeled and whole
2 small white turnips, cubed
450 g/1 lb new potatoes
120 g/4 oz new peas or French beans

1. Sprinkle the lamb cubes with salt and
pepper, then with half the sugar.
2. Melt the butter in a large flameproof
casserole. Add the meat and fry until
browned. Reduce the heat and add the
onion, carrots and garlic. Cook until lightly
browned. Stir in the flour, then the wine.
3. Add the tomato purée to the casserole
then slowly add the beef stock, stirring
constantly. Add the bouquets garnis and
bring to the boil. Remove from the heat.
Preheat the oven to 200°C/400°F/Gas 6.
4. Heat the oil in a frying pan. Add the
shallots and turnips and fry until lightly
browned, sprinkling them with the remaining sugar. Tip into the casserole, cover
and put into the oven for 20 minutes.
5. Add the new potatoes and continue
cooking for a further 1–1¼ hours adding
the peas or beans 20 minutes before the
end. To drink, try a light dry red wine.

Lamb korma

Serves 4

3 tbsp sunflower oil
1 large onion, finely chopped
2 cloves garlic, finely chopped
750 g/1½ lb boned leg of lamb, cut into
 4 cm/1½ in cubes
1 tsp salt
1 tsp garam masala
1 tbsp lemon juice
150 ml/¼ pint natural yogurt
1 tsp chilli powder
1 tsp turmeric
3 bay leaves
¼ tsp ground cloves
seeds of 2 green cardamom pods
285 ml/½ pint chicken stock

1. Heat the oil in a large saucepan. Add the
onion and garlic and fry gently until golden.
Using a slotted spoon, transfer the onion
and garlic to a plate.
2. Add the lamb to the pan and fry, turning
occasionally, until evenly browned. Add the
salt, garam masala, lemon juice and the
fried onion and garlic, and simmer for a few
seconds, stirring.
3. Stir in the yogurt, a spoonful or so at a
time to prevent curdling, until it has all
been added.
4. Add the chilli powder, turmeric, bay
leaves, cloves and cardamom seeds. Add the
stock, stir well and bring to the boil. Simmer very gently, uncovered, for 1½ hours,
or until the lamb cubes are cooked through
and tender.
5. Serve at once, with rice and a selection of
chutneys. To drink, try lager or a light dry
white wine.

Osso buco

Serves 6

butter for frying
1 medium onion, chopped
2 carrots, chopped
2 celery stalks, chopped
2 cloves garlic, mashed
1 bay leaf
4 tbsp olive oil
6 veal shanks, each cut into
    7.5 cm/3 in pieces
flour for coating
1 × 400 g/14 oz tin plum tomatoes
170 ml/6 fl oz white wine
170 ml/6 fl oz chicken stock
1 tsp chopped marjoram
salt and freshly ground black pepper

Garnish

1 clove garlic, finely chopped
1 tbsp grated lemon rind
2 tbsp chopped parsley

1. Preheat the oven to 190°C/375°F/Gas 5. Melt the butter in a large frying pan. Add the onion, carrots, celery, garlic and bay leaf and fry until they are lightly browned. Remove from the pan and set aside.
2. Heat the oil in the same pan. Roll the veal pieces in the flour then brown evenly in the oil for about 5 minutes on each side. Transfer the veal to a large ovenproof casserole dish.
3. Spoon the vegetable mixture over the veal and add the tomatoes (with their juices), wine, stock, marjoram and salt and pepper. Cover the casserole and put into the oven for 1½–1¾ hours or until tender.
4. To prepare the garnish, put the chopped garlic, lemon rind and parsley into a small saucepan with about 120 ml/4 fl oz of cooking juices from the veal. Simmer for about 5 minutes, stirring constantly. A few minutes before the Osso Buco is due to be removed from the oven, add the garnish to the casserole.
5. Serve on a bed of rice or noodles. A light dry red Italian wine would go well here.

Stuffed veal and cheese rolls

Serves 4

4 veal escalopes, beaten out thin then
    halved
4 slices cooked ham, halved
8 thin slices of Gruyère cheese
1 clove garlic, mashed
1 tsp rubbed sage
salt and freshly ground black pepper
flour for dusting
olive oil for frying
120 ml/4 fl oz dry white wine

1. Arrange the veal escalope halves on a flat work surface. Top with a ½ slice ham, then a slice of Gruyère. Mash the garlic and sage together and sprinkle a little over each of the escalopes. Season to taste.
2. Roll up the meat to form a sausage, and tie with thread or secure with a wooden cocktail stick. Dust with flour.
3. Heat the oil in a large frying pan. Add the veal rolls and fry for 5–8 minutes, turning them from time to time, until they are evenly browned. Add the wine, reduce the heat, cover the pan and cook for 12–15 minutes, or until the meat is cooked through and tender.
4. Remove from the pan and carefully remove the string or sticks. Arrange the rolls with their juices over a bed of colourful cooked vegetables such as peas, tomatoes and mushrooms. To drink, try a light dry red wine or a crisp dry white wine.

Pork with peppers and ginger

Serves 2

2 tbsp sunflower oil
¼ medium onion, sliced
few slices of green pepper
1 large or 3–4 small mushrooms, sliced
salt and freshly ground black pepper
5 cm/2 in piece of fresh root ginger, peeled
and chopped
225 g/8 oz pork fillet, trimmed, skinned
and cut into strips
1 tbsp medium or dry sherry
1 tbsp sweet and sour Hong Kong sauce

1. Heat the oil in a frying pan. Add the onion and fry until lightly browned. Add the green pepper slices and stir, then the mushrooms and seasoning to taste, still stirring. Using a slotted spoon, remove the ingredients from the pan and set aside.
2. Add the pork pieces to the pan and fry gently until they seal themselves on all sides – use a little more oil if you need it. Stir-fry for a few minutes.
3. Return the vegetable mixture to the pan, stirring, then stir in the sherry and sweet and sour sauce. Simmer gently until the pork is cooked and tender, about 5 minutes.
4. Serve at once. To drink, try a medium dry white wine.

Pork with orange sauce

Serves 4

750 g/1 ½ lb pork fillet
2 oranges
60 g/2 oz butter
60 ml/2 fl oz orange liqueur
watercress

1. Trim the pork of excess fat and cut into 2.5 cm/1 inch rounds.
2. Using a potato peeler, remove the rind of 1 orange and cut it into matchstick strips. Squeeze the juice of both oranges.
3. Melt the butter in a frying pan. Add the pork to the pan in batches and fry 2–3 minutes on each side. Transfer the pork to a plate and set aside.
4. Add the orange juice to the pan and simmer for 2–3 minutes. Add the orange strips and cook until the sauce begins to caramelize. Remove the pan from the heat. Put the pork and any juices that have collected on the plate into the pan, with the orange liqueur. Return the pan to the heat and cook for one more minute.
5. Serve garnished with watercress. A medium sweet white wine or a dry sparkling white wine would be excellent with this dish.

LEFT: Pork with peppers and ginger;
RIGHT: Pork with orange sauce

Pork pojarsky

Serves 4 (about 4-5 each)

120 g/4 oz fresh breadcrumbs
120 ml/4 fl oz milk
1.25 kg/2 ½ lb lean pork, put through the
*   mincer twice*
1 egg
½ tsp grated nutmeg
1 tsp salt
freshly ground black pepper
60 g/2 oz butter plus extra for frying
85–120 ml/3–4 fl oz whipping
*   cream*
flour for coating

Smitane sauce

15 g/½ oz butter
1 tbsp chopped onion
150 ml/¼ pint dry white wine
600 ml/1 pint sour cream
juice of ¼ lemon

1. Put the breadcrumbs in a large bowl and stir in the milk. Mix in the minced pork, egg, nutmeg, salt and black pepper to taste. Melt the 60 g/2 oz butter and mix in along with the cream.
2. Flour a board. Take a large handful – about 85–120 g/3–4 oz of the mixture and pat together with both hands. Place on the board and shape to look like a lamb cutlet. Flour the edges as well as the top and bottom. Set aside on a tray while you make the sauce.
3. To make the sauce, melt the butter in a saucepan. Add the onion and fry until golden. Pour in the wine and bring to the boil. Continue boiling until the liquid is reduced by two-thirds. Stir in the sour cream and boil for several minutes to thicken the sauce slightly. Remove the pan from the heat and pour the sauce through a strainer. Stir the lemon juice into the strained sauce and return it to the saucepan. Let the sauce simmer very gently while you fry the pojarskys.
4. Melt some butter in a frying pan. Add the pojarskys and fry, turning them occasionally, for 12–14 minutes or until they are cooked through and golden brown. Serve with the Smitane sauce poured over. To drink, try a medium dry white or a soft medium pink wine.

Pork fillet sunshine

Serves 4

800 g/1 ¾ lb pork fillet
85 g/3 oz butter
4 tbsp clear honey
4 tbsp dark thick soy sauce
60 g/2 oz flaked almonds, toasted

1. Trim the pork of excess fat and cut into 12 equal pieces. Turn each piece on its side and, using a meat tenderizer, bash the meat into little round patties.
2. Melt the butter in a large saucepan. Add the pork to the pan in batches and fry for 2 minutes on each side, removing the slices as they are cooked. When all the slices have been cooked, return them to the frying pan.
3. Add the honey and soy sauce. Stir and cook to reduce and thicken the sauce, being careful not to burn the honey. Just before the end of the cooking time, add the almonds.
4. Serve at once with rice or noodles. To drink, try a medium dry white wine or a soft, slightly sparkling rosé.

Pork Vallée d'Auge

The area of Normandy known as the Vallée d'Auge produces several delicate dishes based on a combination of apples and Calvados, an apple brandy which is produced locally. This recipe can be adapted for veal, turkey or chicken escalopes – if you are using these, allow one veal or chicken escalope per person and two turkey escalopes.

Serves 4

2 pork fillets, each about 340 g/12 oz in weight
45 g/1 ½ oz butter
2 medium eating apples, peeled, cored and sliced
2 tbsp Calvados
85 ml/3 fl oz whipping cream

1. Trim, skin and cut each fillet into 6 equal pieces. Beat and flatten out, then set them aside.
2. Melt the butter in a large frying pan. Add the apple slices and fry until just soft. Using a slotted spoon, remove from the pan and set aside. Add the pork to the pan, in batches, and fry gently for a few minutes on each side. Stir in the Calvados and increase the heat.
3. Pour in the cream and when it just bubbles reduce the heat. Simmer for a minute or two and add the apples and any cooking juices and simmer for 3–5 minutes until the sauce thickens slightly. (If you overcook the sauce will separate; if this happens, however, you can add a little more cream to bring the sauce back to life.)
4. To serve, arrange the pork on a serving plate and spoon over the sauce. Top with the apples. To drink, try cider or a crisp dry white wine.

Cold roast pork with prunes and pine nuts

Serves 6

1 × 200 g/7 oz tin prunes
1.5 kg/3 lb boned loin of pork
1 tbsp pine nuts
pinch of dried thyme
1 tsp oil
salt and freshly ground black pepper
85 ml/3 fl oz dry or medium sherry

1. Preheat the oven to 190°C/375°F/ Gas 5. Drain the prunes and remove the stones, then pat dry.
2. Wash and dry the pork. Open out the meat and lay it flat on your work surface. Place about 12 prunes along the centre leaving 2.5 cm/1 inch free at each end. Sprinkle over the pine nuts and then the thyme.
3. Roll up the pork and tie in 6 places with string or strong thread to hold it together. Brush all over with the oil, rub in a little salt and sprinkle over some pepper.
4. Put the pork into a baking tin containing about 1.5 cm/½ inch water. Put into the oven and roast for 30 minutes. Baste with the sherry and continue cooking for 1½–2 hours or until cooked through.
5. Leave to cool. When quite cold remove the crackling, cut the meat into slices and serve. A medium sweet white wine or a soft medium pink wine would make an excellent accompaniment to this dish.

Gammon with Cumberland sauce

Serves 4–6

1·25 kg/2½ lb gammon, soaked for
  24 hours in cold water
1 tbsp soft brown sugar
10 whole cloves
285 ml/½ pint cider

Cumberland sauce

2 oranges
225 g/8 oz redcurrant jelly
1 tbsp cornflour, mixed to a paste with
  2–3 tbsp water
120 ml/4 fl oz port

1. First make the sauce. Using a potato peeler, thinly peel the oranges and cut the rind into matchstick strips. Put them into a saucepan with a little water to cover and bring to the boil. Boil for a few minutes, and then strain. Repeat this twice. Remove the orange rind from the pan and set aside.

Gammon with Cumberland sauce

2. Squeeze the juice from the oranges into a second saucepan and add the redcurrant jelly. Heat over gentle heat, stirring until the jelly dissolves. Stir in the cornflour mixture until it has dissolved and the sauce is smooth. Stir in the port and simmer for 2–3 minutes, until the sauce has thickened and is smooth. Remove from the heat and stir in the orange strips. Set aside.

3. Preheat the oven to 190°C/375°F/Gas 5. Drain the gammon and put into a large pan. Cover with water and bring to the boil. Boil for 12 minutes, then remove from the heat and drain. Remove the skin, but not the fat. Allow to cool slightly.

4. Stand the gammon on its side in a baking tin. Rub the top and the top half of the sides with the sugar, then push the cloves through the sugar into the meat. Pour the cider around the gammon but not over the top.

5. Bake in the oven for 1–1¼ hours, basting the top of the gammon with the cider after the first 20 minutes.

6. Serve sliced, with the cool sauce. A soft medium pink wine is excellent with this dish.

Kidneys in mustard

Kidneys in mustard

Serves 4

60 g/2 oz butter
200 ml/7 fl oz dry cider
*1 tsp each of Meaux, Dijon and English
    mustards*
1 tsp green peppercorns (in brine)
*1 × 425 g/15 oz can button mushrooms,
    drained*
salt and freshly ground black pepper
*16 lambs' kidneys, halved, fat and veins
    removed*
120 ml/4 fl oz single cream
*1 tbsp chopped parsley, plus extra to
    garnish*

1. Melt the butter in a large saucepan. Pour over the cider and cook for 3 minutes until it has reduced somewhat. Stir in the mustards, green peppercorns, mushrooms and seasoning to taste. Cook for 2–3 minutes to allow the flavours to blend.

2. Add the kidneys to the pan and cook for 12–15 minutes, turning occasionally, or until cooked through. Stir in the cream and parsley and simmer very gently until the sauce thickens but does not begin to separate.

3. Garnish with the parsley and serve over rice. To drink, try a medium dry or medium sweet white wine.

Chicken fricassee

Serves 4

4 chicken legs
4 chicken thighs
120 g/4 oz butter
16 shallots, peeled
170 g/6 oz carrots, sliced into ovals
85 g/3 oz mushrooms, sliced
flour for coating
60 ml/2 fl oz dry white wine
200 ml/7 fl oz chicken stock
salt and freshly ground black pepper
1 bouquet garni
2 bay leaves
4 tbsp cream

1. Preheat the oven to 220°C/425°F/Gas 7. Wash the chicken pieces and wipe dry with kitchen paper towels.
2. Melt the butter in a large frying pan. Add the shallots and carrots and fry until browned. Add the mushrooms and fry for 1–2 minutes. Using a slotted spoon, transfer the vegetables to a plate. Set aside and keep warm.
3. Coat the chicken pieces in flour, shaking off any excess, and add them to the frying pan. Fry, turning occasionally, until they are evenly browned. Return the vegetables to the pan. Slowly pour in wine, shaking the pan as you do so. Add the stock, season to taste and bring to the boil. Remove the pan from the heat.
4. Transfer the contents of the frying pan to a casserole dish. Add the bouquet garni and the bay leaves and put the casserole into the oven. Cook for 25–30 minutes or until the chicken is tender.
5. Remove the bouquet garni and bay leaves and stir in the cream before serving. Serve with new potatoes and a mixed salad and, to drink, try a crisp dry white wine or a light dry red.

Szechuan chicken

Szechuan is the most westerly province of China and produces some lovely recipes, often with quite a hot chilli base. The quantities given below will serve four people only if the dish is served with rice or Chinese noodles and as part of a larger Chinese meal.

Serves 4

2 tbsp sesame oil
1 medium onion, chopped
2 carrots, thinly sliced lengthways then diagonally into strips
2 tsp grated fresh root ginger
4 pieces of sliced stem ginger in vinegar, sliced even finer
2 tbsp dry sherry
2 tsp red wine vinegar
4 boned chicken breasts, each about 170–200 g/6–7 oz, cut into strips
4–5 water chestnuts, drained and sliced
2 tsp sesame seeds
3 tbsp light soy sauce
1 tbsp Szechuan chilli and tomato sauce, or to taste

1. Heat the oil in a wok or large frying pan. Add the onion and carrots and stir-fry for 2 minutes, then add the grated ginger and stir-fry for 1 minute. Now stir in the stem ginger for 1 minute, followed by the sherry and red wine vinegar – cook for 1 minute more. Add the chicken pieces and cook, stirring, for 3 minutes. Stir in the water chestnuts, sesame seeds and soy sauce and fry for 1 minute. Lastly add the chilli sauce and stir-fry for 1–2 minutes.
2. Serve over a bed of rice or noodles. To drink, try a light medium dry white wine such as Liebfraumilch or riesling or chilled lager.

Chicken with ginger sauce

Serves 4
60 g/2 oz butter
4 boned chicken breasts, each about
  170 g/6 oz
3 tbsp ginger wine
170 ml/6 fl oz whipping or single
  cream
salt and freshly ground pepper

1. Melt the butter in a frying pan. Add the chicken breasts and fry for about 5 minutes, turning occasionally. Stir in the ginger wine and simmer for 5 minutes, stirring from time to time until it becomes slightly caramelized.
2. Add the cream and seasoning and simmer for a further 10 minutes or until the chicken is cooked through and the sauce has thickened.
3. Serve at once with a selection of crisp vegetables and rice. A medium dry white wine would be a good accompaniment to this dish.

Chicken tarragon

Take care that the whipping cream does not separate when it is added to the pan in this dish – if it does, then add a little more, stirring vigorously until it all amalgamates again.

Serves 4
60 g/2 oz butter
150 ml/¼ pint dry white wine
4 chicken breasts, each about
  120–170 g/4–6 oz
120 ml/4 fl oz whipping cream
1 ½ tablespoons chopped tarragon or
  2 teaspoons dried tarragon

1. Melt the butter in a frying pan large enough to take the four chicken breasts in one layer. Add the white wine and heat until hot.
2. Place the chicken pieces in the pan, flat side down, and simmer for about 5 minutes, shaking the pan occasionally. Turn over and cook in the same way on the other side. Make sure the heat is not too high and that the meat does not brown; it should be kept white for this recipe.
3. Turn the chicken again then stir in the cream. Bring to the boil and add the tarragon.
4. Turn down the heat so that the sauce is just bubbling (too high and the cream will separate). Keep cooking until the sauce has reduced and thickened.
5. Serve with just enough sauce to cover the chicken. A crisp dry white French wine would be an excellent accompaniment to Chicken tarragon.

Crispy duck

This is a superb dish. In China they have special ovens and very special routines for hanging and coating their ducks. This is my easy and much simplified recipe.

Serves 4

1 × 2 kg/4 lb oven-ready duck
1 tbsp caster sugar dissolved in
*   8 tbsp boiling water*

Pancakes

285 g/10 oz plain flour
250 ml/9 fl oz boiling water
2 tbsp sesame oil

Filling

1 bottle Peking Duck Sauce
½ cucumber, peeled, seeded and finely
*   sliced into 7.5 cm/3 inch strips*
1 bunch spring onions, finely sliced

1. If the duck is frozen defrost it. Hang the duck by its feet in a draught to dry overnight or, if that is not possible, use a hair dryer: lay the duck on a table and place the hair dryer a few inches away, turning to dry evenly. When the duck begins to dry brush it all over with the sugar solution. Dry the duck again and brush once again with the sweetened water. This will take approximately 2 hours.

2. Before roasting the duck make the pancakes. Sift the flour into a mixing bowl. Gradually add the boiling water, beating well with a wooden spoon. When a dough is formed turn it out and knead well for 5 minutes. Cover the dough with a damp cloth and let it rest for 15 minutes. Then repeat the kneading. Shape the dough into a roll about 5 cm/2 inches in diameter. Cut the roll into 16 or 18 pieces. Then, on a floured surface, pat and roll out each piece into a pancake 15 cm/6 inches in diameter.

Brush the tops of the pancakes with the oil and put 2 pancakes together, dry sides outside. Press them gently together.

3. Keep a damp tea cloth by the side of the stove. Put a heavy frying pan over a moderate to low heat. When the pan is hot put in a double pancake and cook for 2–3 minutes. When brown spots appear on the underside turn the pancakes over and cook for a further 2–3 minutes. Be careful not to let them burn. Take out the pancakes, separate them and pile them on the damp tea cloth. When all the pancakes are done fold over the teacloth and set aside while you roast the duck.

4. Preheat the oven to 200°C/400°F/Gas 6. Place the duck on a rack with a drip tray underneath and put into the oven for 15 minutes. Reduce the temperature to 190°C/375°F/Gas 5 and roast the duck for 1½ hours or until it is tender and the skin is very crisp.

5. Thirty minutes before the duck is ready, bring some water to the boil in a large saucepan. Put the pancakes in the tea towel in a colander and place over the boiling water. Reduce the heat slightly and steam for 15 minutes until heated through.

6. Remove the duck from the oven and slice off the skin. Lay the skin pieces on a heated serving dish. Then cut the duck into thin slices and put these on another heated serving dish. Arrange the filling ingredients on a large serving plate. Fold each pancake in half and pile on a heated plate.

7. To serve, spread a pancake with the Peking Duck sauce, sprinkle with cucumber and spring onions and place pieces of duck skin and meat over them. Fold the pancake and eat with the fingers. To drink, try a soft medium pink wine, a medium dry white or a light dry red.

Crispy duck

Creamed meat balls

Serves 4–6

*750 g/1 ½ lb mixed minced meat
  (pork, beef, etc)
3 dashes of Worcestershire sauce
freshly ground black pepper
1 egg, beaten
1 tbsp mixed dried herbs
plain flour for coating
bacon fat or dripping for frying*

Mushroom sauce

*1 medium onion, chopped
60 g/2 oz mushrooms, finely chopped
1 tbsp tomato purée
1 tbsp flour
600 ml/1 pint strong beef stock
1 tbsp mixed dried herbs
salt and freshly ground black pepper*

1. Mix together all the ingredients for the meatballs, except the flour and fat, in a large bowl. Using your hands, form the mixture into about 20 walnut-sized balls and roll in the flour, shaking off any excess.
2. Melt the fat or dripping in a large frying pan. Add the meatballs, in batches, and fry until they are well and evenly browned. Using a slotted spoon, transfer them to a large ovenproof dish as they brown. Pre-heat the oven to 180°C/350°F/Gas 4.
3. To make the sauce, add the onion and mushrooms to the fat in the frying pan, adding extra if necessary. Fry gently until the onion is soft. Stir in the tomato purée and flour and cook for 3–4 minutes, stirring constantly. Pour over the stock and bring to the boil. Reduce the heat and simmer for 5 minutes to reduce slightly. Stir in the herbs and season to taste.
4. Pour the sauce over the meatballs, cover and cook in the oven for about 40 minutes. Serve hot. To drink, try a dry white wine.

Rabbit with chestnut purée

Serves 4

*85 g/3 oz butter
1 medium onion, chopped
2 cloves garlic, crushed
1 carrot, sliced
2 bay leaves
1 rabbit, prepared and jointed
120 g/4 oz bacon, rinds removed and
  chopped (optional)
60 g/2 oz flour, seasoned with salt and
  pepper
285 ml/½ pint red wine
12 shallots, peeled and whole
30 g/1 oz green peppercorns
60 g/2 oz mushrooms, sliced
1 bouquet garni
1 tsp dried tarragon
salt and freshly ground pepper
1 × 450 g/16 oz can unsweetened
  chestnut purée
120 ml/4 fl oz cream*

1. Melt the butter in a large saucepan or flameproof casserole. Add the onion and garlic and fry until golden. Add the carrot and bay leaves, then the rabbit and bacon (if used), cooking the rabbit to brown. Stir in the flour until dissolved.
2. Pour in the wine and bring to the boil. Add the shallots, green peppercorns, mushrooms, bouquet garni, tarragon and salt and pepper to taste. Cover and simmer for 1–1¼ hours, or until the rabbit is cooked and tender.
3. Just before serving, beat the chestnut purée with the cream until thick.
4. Transfer the rabbit mixture to a warmed serving platter. Form the chestnut mixture into decorative whirls and use to garnish the outside of the platter.

Forest pie

This dish is called Forest Pie because it contains both venison and wild mushrooms, which you can buy dried, in packets. Dried mushrooms are expensive, however, and can be difficult to obtain – substitute about 60 g/2 oz fresh button or field mushrooms if you cannot find them and omit the soaking.

Serves 6

450 g/1 lb lean venison, trimmed and cubed
450 g/1 lb chuck steak, cubed
225 g/8 oz ox kidneys, trimmed, cored and cubed
60 g/2 oz streaky bacon, rinds removed and chopped
60 g/2 oz butter
1 large onion, chopped
1 tbsp flour
340 ml/12 fl oz red wine
2 cloves garlic, crushed
1 bouquet garni
salt and freshly ground black pepper
handful of dried mushrooms (ceps for preference), soaked overnight
425 g/15 oz frozen puff pastry, thawed

Marinade

340 ml/12 fl oz red wine
120 ml/4 fl oz vegetable oil
1 onion, chopped
1 carrot, chopped
2 cloves garlic, crushed
2 bay leaves
1 bouquet garni
6 peppercorns
1/4 tsp salt

1. To make the marinade, combine all the ingredients in a large shallow bowl. Add the venison, beef and kidney pieces, turning them over to coat. Set aside in the refrigerator at least overnight, and preferably for 24 hours.

2. Using a slotted spoon, remove the meat from the marinade and pat dry with absorbent paper towels. Set aside. Reserve the marinade.

3. Fry the bacon in a large heavy-based saucepan until the fat starts to run. Put in the butter and, when it has melted, add the onion. Sweat until it becomes translucent. Stir in the flour until it browns, then add the meat, stirring until it too becomes golden brown.

4. Add the red wine and strained marinade liquid. The sauce must just cover the meat so add a little water if necessary. Stir in the garlic and bouquet garni. Season to taste. Bring to the boil, reduce the heat, cover the pan and simmer for 1 hour.

5. Add the mushrooms and their soaking liquid (if using dried mushrooms – do not add extra liquid if substituting fresh). Simmer for a further 1–1½ hours or until the meat is tender. Remove the bouquet garni and adjust the seasoning to taste.

6. Preheat the oven to 200°C/400°F/Gas 6. Thirty minutes before the dish is cooked, roll out the pastry to 1 cm/½ inch thick and cut out a round 11.25 cm/4½ inches in diameter. Using a sharp knife score a circle in the top about 2.5 cm/1 inch from the edge. Put the pastry on a dampened baking tray and bake for 25 minutes. If the pastry begins to brown too quickly reduce the oven temperature a little.

7. To serve, transfer the meat to a deep pie dish or decorative casserole and top with the puff pastry 'top hat'. A full soft red wine such as Côtes-du-Rhône or Barbera would be excellent here.

VEGETABLE AND VEGETARIAN DISHES

Aubergine and tomato bake

Serves 4–6

2 large aubergines, sliced
salt and freshly ground black pepper
butter and oil for frying
1 large onion, finely sliced
1 clove garlic, crushed
1 × 400 g/14 oz tin tomatoes, sieved
1 tbsp tomato purée
1 tsp chopped basil or ½ tsp dried basil
½ tsp sugar
150 ml/¼ pint natural yogurt
30 g/1 oz Parmesan cheese, grated
30 g/1 oz fresh white breadcrumbs

1. Put the aubergine slices in layers in a colander, sprinkling each layer with salt. Put a plate on top and weigh it down. Leave for 30 minutes then rinse thoroughly and dry with absorbent paper towels.
2. Preheat the oven to 180°C/350°F/Gas 4. Heat a knob of butter and a tablespoon of oil in a large frying pan. When the butter foams, arrange a layer of aubergine slices in the pan and fry, turning occasionally, until browned on both sides. Using a slotted spoon, remove the slices from the pan and drain on absorbent paper towels. Fry the remaining slices in the same way, adding more butter and oil as necessary.
3. In the same pan, fry the onion and garlic until golden. Stir in the tomatoes, tomato purée, basil, sugar and salt and pepper to taste. When bubbling, reduce the heat and simmer for 5 minutes to thicken the sauce slightly.

Aubergine and tomato bake

4. Put one-third of the aubergine slices into a shallow ovenproof dish. Pour half the tomato sauce over the slices and half the yogurt on top of the sauce. Repeat these 3 layers once more and put the remaining aubergine slices on top. Sprinkle with the grated Parmesan and the breadcrumbs. Bake in the oven for 30 minutes or until the top is golden brown and bubbling.
5. Serve at once, with salad and crusty bread as a light main dish, or as a substantial side dish. To drink, try a light red wine or a soft medium pink wine.

Tortellini Galvani

Serves 4

450 g/1 lb tortellini
30 g/1 oz butter
1 medium onion, finely sliced
225 g/8 oz button mushrooms, finely sliced
salt and freshly ground black pepper
1 tsp dried savory
2 tsp plus some extra grated Parmesan
285 ml/½ pint whipping cream

1. Follow the instructions on the packet but undercook the tortellini by 2 minutes. Drain and keep hot.
2. Meanwhile, melt the butter in a frying pan. Add the onion and mushrooms and fry gently until they are soft. Season to taste, then stir in the savory and 2 tsp grated Parmesan.
3. Stir in the cream, then add the tortellini, basting gently with the cream until mixed. Cook gently for 2 minutes to heat through and cook the pasta completely.
4. Serve with extra Parmesan cheese and, to drink, a medium-dry white wine.

Pizza

Serves 4

2 tsp dried active baking yeast
½ tsp sugar
1 tsp salt
170 ml/6 fl oz warm water
400 g/14 oz plain flour, sifted
450 g/1 lb tomatoes, skinned
175 g/6 oz Mozzarella, Cheddar, Edam or
    Gruyère cheese
3 cloves garlic, crushed
large pinch of dried oregano
pinch of dried basil
salt and freshly ground black pepper
oil for brushing

1. Dissolve the yeast, sugar and salt in the warm water and set aside in a warm place for about 10 minutes or until it is frothy.
2. Place the flour on your working surface and make a well in the centre. Slowly pour in the yeast mixture, mixing it into the flour by hand until you have a smooth ball of dough. Put the dough into a floured bowl, cover and set aside in a warm place for 45–60 minutes or until it has doubled in size.
3. While all this is taking place assemble the topping ingredients: slice the tomatoes and remove the seeds, slice the cheese, have the garlic, herbs and seasonings ready.
4. Preheat the oven to 230°C/450°F/Gas 8. When the dough is risen, knead it for a few minutes then cut into portions, depending on the size of the pizza you plan to cook: halve it for large, cut into 4 for medium and into 6 for small ones. Roll the pieces out on a floured surface to about 5 mm/¼ inch thick, using your thumbs to build up the edges (this will prevent the filling from overflowing during cooking). Brush each pizza base with oil and transfer it to an oiled baking sheet.

5. Arrange the ingredients on top of the pizza, as you prefer – try tomato slices first, topped by cheese slices and with crushed garlic, oregano, basil and seasoning scattered over.
6. Put the baking sheet into the oven and cook for about 12–15 minutes – the time will vary somewhat according to the size of the pizza or pizzas; test with a fork to see if crisp.
7. Serve hot with salad and a crisp dry white wine or lager, or a light red wine such as Chianti or Valpolicella.

Note: The above toppings are only one selection among many possibilities: try, for instance, anchovies, ham strips, capers, olives, mushrooms, salami strips, raisins and peppers – in any combination to suit your taste.

Spinach tart

Serves 6

225 g/8 oz frozen leaf spinach
30 g/1 oz butter
salt and freshly ground pepper
pinch of grated nutmeg
1 tsp lemon juice
225 g/8 oz cottage cheese
4 eggs, beaten
60 g/2 oz Cheddar cheese,
    grated
4 tbsp double cream

Pastry

120 g/4 oz plain wholemeal flour
120 g/4 oz self-raising wholemeal
    flour
½ tsp salt
120 g/4 oz margarine
1 egg yolk
1 tbsp cold water

1. To make the pastry, combine the flours and salt together in a mixing bowl. Add the margarine and rub it in until the mixture resembles fine breadcrumbs. Add the egg yolk and water, and mix to a firm dough. Cover and chill in the refrigerator for 1 hour.

2. Preheat the oven to 190°C/375°F/Gas 5. Lightly grease a 20–23 cm/8–9 inch flan ring and arrange on a baking sheet. Roll out the dough on a floured surface and use to line the flan ring. Prick the bottom with a fork, line with foil or greaseproof paper and weigh down with rice or dried beans. Bake in the oven for 15 minutes. Remove from the oven and lift off the beans or rice and foil or paper and set the pastry aside to allow it to cool.

3. While the pastry is baking, make the filling. Cook the spinach with the butter in a saucepan until thawed and heated through. Stir in seasoning to taste, nutmeg and lemon juice. Remove from the heat and allow to cool slightly.

4. Transfer the spinach to a bowl and beat in the cottage cheese, eggs, grated cheese and cream until well blended. Spoon this mixture into the baked pastry case and cook in the oven for 25–30 minutes, or until the filling is set and the tart is golden brown on top.

5. Serve hot or cold with salad as a lunch or supper dish. A crisp dry Italian white wine or a light dry red wine would be excellent with this dish.

Vegetarian rissoles

We usually serve these little meatless 'hamburgers' with a hot sauce, such as mushroom, tomato and onion or asparagus cream. They freeze well, so make large quantities to have them on hand for quick emergency meals!

Serves 4 (2 rissoles each)

170 g/6 oz Weetabix, crumbled
170 g/6 oz carrots, grated
170 g/6 oz onions, grated
60 g/2 oz flaked almonds, crushed
60 g/2 oz walnuts, finely chopped
2 tsp chopped basil
2 eggs, beaten
120 g/4 oz wholemeal flour
salt and freshly ground pepper
oil for frying
1 egg, beaten with 2 tbsp milk
4 tbsp wholemeal flour
    for coating

1. Put all the ingredients, except the oil, egg mixture and flour for coating into a mixing bowl and beat until well blended. Form into small flat patties, about 1.5 cm/½ inch thick and 7.5 cm/3 inches in diameter. Chill in the refrigerator for 20 minutes or until firm.

2. Put the egg and milk mixture into one shallow bowl and the flour on to a large plate. Dip the patties first in the egg mixture then into the flour, shaking off any excess.

3. Heat the oil in a large frying pan. Add the patties, a few at a time, and cook for about 3 minutes on each side, or until they are brown and crisp.

4. Drain on absorbent paper towels and serve immediately, with the sauce of your choice. A crisp dry white or a soft medium pink wine would complement this dish well.

Vegetable curry

Serve as a vegetarian meal with rice and a selection of other accompaniments (it will serve 2-3 as a main course), or as an accompaniment to a meat curry (see pages 35 and 38) and with a selection of chutneys. Cucumber and mint sambal (see page 70) also makes a good accompaniment to this dish.

Serves 4–6

2 tbsp sunflower oil
1 medium onion, chopped
1 tsp ground cumin
1 tsp ground coriander
1 tsp garam masala
1 tin Rogan Josh medium hot curry sauce
2 carrots, quartered
2 celery stalks, cut into 5 cm/2 inch lengths
60 g/2 oz french beans
120 g/4 oz okra, topped and tailed
½ cauliflower, cut into small florets
1 green pepper, seeded and sliced
430 ml/¾ pint chicken stock
salt (optional)

1. Heat the oil in a large saucepan. Add the onion and fry for about 5 minutes, stirring constantly and being careful not to let it burn.

2. Add the cumin, coriander and garam masala and fry for 1–2 minutes. Stir well to mix and add the Rogan Josh curry sauce.

3. Add the vegetables and fry for 5 minutes over medium heat. Stir well again and then slowly add the stock. Simmer, uncovered, until the vegetables are cooked. Taste the curry and add salt if necessary. Transfer to a serving dish and keep in a warm oven until ready to serve. Garnish with fresh corian-

LEFT: Vegetable curry; RIGHT: Cucumber and mint sambal (see page 70)

der. Curries are usually served with lager rather than wine – if you prefer wine, however, then stick to a light medium or dry white wine such as a German or Alsatian Sylvaner or Riesling.

Note: Other vegetables such as broccoli, leeks, swedes, mushrooms, broad beans, peas and potatoes may be used instead of or in addition to any of the vegetables in this recipe.

57

Gratin of artichokes

Serves 4

6 large artichokes or 18 tinned artichoke
    bottoms
juice of 1 lemon
salt
85 g/3 oz butter
60 g/2 oz flour
430 ml/¾ pint milk
120 g/4 oz Gruyère or strong Cheddar
    cheese, grated
1 tsp English mustard
60 g/2 oz mushrooms, sliced
1 clove garlic, chopped (optional)
60 g/2 oz ham, diced
2 pinches of celery salt
freshly ground black pepper
1 tbsp grated Parmesan cheese

1. To prepare the artichokes if you are using
fresh ones: using a sharp stainless steel
knife, cut off the stalks and then the outer
leaves. Then cut off the remaining leaves
surrounding the heart. Using a teaspoon
remove the choke (the fibrous part). Put
1.2 litres/2 pints of cold water in a bowl with
the lemon juice. As the artichoke hearts are
prepared drop them into the acidulated
water to prevent discoloration. When all are
.done put them into a saucepan of water, add
a little salt and simmer for 15–20 minutes.
2. Meanwhile, melt two-thirds of the butter
in a saucepan. Stir in the flour and remove
from the heat. Slowly add the milk, stirring
constantly. Return the pan to the heat and
slowly bring the sauce to the simmer, stirring until it is smooth and thick. Remove
from the heat and stir in the Gruyère or
Cheddar cheese until it melts. Stir in the
mustard.
3. Melt the remaining butter in a frying
pan. Add the mushrooms and garlic, if you
are using it, and fry until soft. Stir in the

ham. Mix the mushrooms and ham into the
cheese sauce. Then the celery salt and
pepper.
4. Preheat the oven to 230°C/450°F/Gas 8.
Drain the artichokes and put them into a
casserole dish large enough to accommo-
date them in one layer. Fill each artichoke
heart with some of the sauce. Sprinkle the
top with the Parmesan cheese and bake in
the oven for 10–15 minutes or until nicely
browned.

Spanish omelette

Serves 4–6

6 tbsp olive oil
450 g/1 lb potatoes, peeled and sliced
1 tsp salt
1 large onion, sliced
4 large eggs

1. Heat the oil in a large frying pan. When
hot add the potato slices and fry for 5
minutes, turning occasionally. Sprinkle
over half the salt. Stir in the onion and
continue to fry, over low heat and stirring
frequently, for about 30 minutes or until
the potatoes are cooked through and
brown.
2. Beat the eggs with the remaining salt in a
large bowl.
3. When the potatoes are cooked, tip them
into the bowl with the eggs and stir with a
wooden spoon. Return the mixture to the
frying pan adding extra oil first, if necessary. Fry the mixture for 3–4 minutes.
4. To turn the omelette, cover the top of the
pan with a large plate then, holding both
firmly, quickly reverse the two. Now slide
the omelette back into the pan and cook the
other side until it has browned.
5. Serve hot or cold. To drink, try a medium
sweet white wine.

Hungarian marrow

Marrow is the traditional vegetable used for this popular Hungarian dish, but when this is not available, large courgettes make an excellent substitute. It is equally delicious served hot or cold.

Serves 4

1 × 2 kg/4 lb marrow, peeled and
    seeded
1 tbsp salt
45 g/1 ½ oz butter
1 large onion, chopped
1 tbsp flour
85 g/3 oz sweet-sour gherkins,
    chopped
85 ml/3 fl oz jar juice from gherkins
pinch of dried basil
150 ml/¼ pint sour cream
salt and freshly ground black
    pepper

1. Grate the marrow lengthways into a colander, sprinkle with the salt and cover with a tea towel. Put a plate on top and weigh it down. Allow to drain until the pulp has reduced by about half.
2. Melt the butter in a small saucepan. Add the onion and fry gently until soft. Do not brown. Stir in the flour to make a smooth paste, then stir in the gherkins, slowly adding the juice after the gherkins themselves are blended. Cook gently for a few minutes.
3. Transfer the mixture to a blender and purée. Return to the saucepan and simmer very gently until hot. Stir in the basil and sour cream and season to taste with salt and pepper.
4. Put the marrow into the sauce, stir carefully and cook for a few minutes. Do not overcook – marrow and courgettes require very little cooking.

Vol au vents of creamed quails' eggs

Serves 4

4 large frozen vol-au-vent cases
120 g/4 oz mushrooms, finely
    sliced
30 g/1 oz butter
½ tsp dried oregano
16 quails' eggs
4 tinned artichoke bottoms,
    drained

White sauce

30 g/1 oz butter
30 g/1 oz flour
285 ml/½ pint milk
salt and freshly ground black
    pepper

1. Heat up the vol au vents in the pre-heated oven according to the packet instructions.
2. To make the white sauce, melt the butter in a small saucepan. Remove from the heat and stir in the flour to make a smooth paste. Slowly add the milk, stirring all the time. Return to the heat and simmer gently, stirring constantly, for a further 2-3 minutes or until the sauce thickens. Season to taste with salt and pepper.
3. Sweat the mushrooms in the butter until translucent, then stir them, with the oregano and eggs, into the white sauce. Remove from the heat.
4. Remove the vol au vents from the oven and insert an artichoke bottom into each one. Return to the oven to heat through for a few minutes.
5. Remove the quails' eggs from the sauce and arrange them on top of the artichokes. Cover with sauce and brown slightly under a hot grill. Serve as a substantial starter or as a light lunch or supper dish.

Mixed vegetables with cream

Serves 6

Start with several of the basic vegetables:
*a carrot, swede, cauliflower, parsnip, a
small turnip – one or two of each will do,
or buy a 450g/1 lb ready-prepared
vegetable stew pack*

Then add whatever is available in season:
*a handful of green beans, some peas (do
not use frozen), a broccoli head, a leek or
two, celeriac (you will not need all of it but
any left over will keep for days in the
larder), kohlrabi, sweetcorn and any
others you happen to fancy. (The only
vegetables that are not suitable are
Brussels sprouts and cabbage, which go
mushy.)*
*salt and freshly ground pepper
about 120 ml/4 fl oz single cream
pinch of grated nutmeg (optional)*

1. Prepare and cut the vegetables into even
walnut-sized pieces. Rinse in cold water
then add the root vegetables to boiling
salted water and cook for about 3–5 minutes. Add any remaining vegetables and
cook for 2–4 minutes or until they are all
just tender.
2. Drain, then transfer to a warmed serving
dish. Season to taste and add sufficient
cream just to coat the vegetables. If you
like, you can add a touch of grated nutmeg
as well.

Mixed vegetables with cream

Stuffed onions

Stuffed onions

If you want something different to accompany your roasts, then try this – although it can equally easily be served on its own as a snack.

Serves 4

4 large onions, peeled
45 g/1 ½ oz butter
1 tbsp finely chopped celery
1 tbsp finely chopped parsley
2 tbsp finely chopped
   mushrooms
120 g/4 oz fresh breadcrumbs
1 tsp dried savory
½ tsp lemon and pepper
   seasoning
pinch of salt
2 tsp red wine or stock

1. Boil the onions for about 20 minutes or until just soft. Drain and cut 1.5 cm/½ inch from the tops. Press out centres with your fingers, then chop them finely – you will need about 2 tbsp for the stuffing.
2. Melt 30 g/1 oz of the butter in a small frying pan. Add the chopped onion and fry gently for about 30 seconds. Add the celery, parsley, mushrooms, breadcrumbs (reserve some of the breadcrumbs for sprinkling), savory and seasoning and fry gently for 3–4 minutes. Stir in the wine or stock. Cook for 2–3 minutes, then remove the pan from the heat.
3. Preheat the oven to 190°C/375°F/Gas 5. Arrange the onions on a greased baking sheet. Spoon the stuffing mixture into the centres and sprinkle the reserved breadcrumbs over the tops. Dot with the remaining butter. Cover and bake in the oven for about 30-40 minutes, or until cooked.

Shredded leeks

Serves 4

450 g/1 lb leeks
30 g/1 oz butter
60 ml/2 fl oz single cream
salt and freshly ground black pepper

1. Top and tail the leeks. Slice them in half lengthways then cut them crossways very thinly into slices. Put them into a colander and rinse thoroughly under cold running water. Leave to dry a little.
2. Put the leeks into a saucepan with the butter and sweat them in their own juice over a moderate heat for 5 minutes.
3. Stir in the cream. Reduce briskly for 1 minute. Stir, season to taste and serve.

Crispy fried cabbage

Serves 4

225 g/8 oz cabbage, green or savoy
oil for deep frying
sea salt

1. Cut out the stalk and pull each leaf off separately. Cut out the main vein and any other veins that are thick.
2. Slice the leaves very thinly, into matchstick strips about 10 cm/4 inches long. Wash, drain and pat very dry.
3. Fill a deep-frying pan about one-third full with oil and heat to about 180°C/350°F or, if you do not have a deep-frying thermometer, drop in a cube of stale bread. If it browns in 50 seconds the temperature will be about right. Using a deep-frying basket, deep-fry the cabbage, in batches, for a few seconds until crispy but not browned. Drain on absorbent paper towels and sprinkle with sea salt just before serving.

Colcannon Galvani

Serves 4–6

1 tbsp bacon fat
3 rashers streaky bacon, rinds removed, and chopped
1 medium onion, chopped
750 g/1 ½ lb cabbage, cooked and shredded
750 g/1 ½ lb potatoes, boiled and mashed
salt and freshly ground black pepper
30 g/1 oz butter, diced

1. Preheat the oven to 200°C/400°F/Gas 6. Melt the bacon fat in a frying pan. Add the bacon and onion and fry gently until the bacon is cooked.
2. Put the cabbage and potatoes into a large bowl. Tip in the bacon and onion and season to taste. Mix well and transfer to a shallow ovenproof dish. Smooth the top, dot with the butter and bake for 30 minutes or until browned and crisp.

Brussels sprout purée

Serves 4–6

450 g/1 lb Brussels sprouts, trimmed
30 g/1 oz butter
75 ml/2 ½ fl oz whipping cream
¼ tsp grated nutmeg
salt and freshly ground black pepper

1. Boil or steam the sprouts until they are cooked but still crisp. Drain and put them through a medium mincer.
2. Melt the butter in a saucepan. Stir in the cream and nutmeg. Add the sprout purée and salt and pepper to taste. Stir well and heat through.

Galette potatoes

Serves 4

450 g/1 lb potatoes, peeled
120 g/4 oz cream cheese
1 tbsp grated Parmesan cheese
1 tbsp chopped parsley
60 g/2 oz butter
1 level tbsp ground almonds
salt and freshly ground black
pepper
oil for deep frying or butter for shallow
frying

Coating

2 tbsp flour
1 egg, beaten
3 tbsp medium matzo meal
1 tbsp flaked almonds

1. Cook the potatoes and purée them with the cream cheese, Parmesan, parsley, butter and ground almonds. Season to taste with salt and pepper.
2. Form the mixture into 7.5 cm/3 inch flat cakes.
3. Put each of the coating ingredients on to separate plates. Dip the cakes first into the flour, then into the beaten egg and finally into the matzo meal and almonds, shaking off any excess.
4. Either deep fry or sauté in butter until the cakes are golden brown. Drain on paper towels before serving.

Gratin dauphinoise

Serves 4

450 g/1 lb large potatoes, cut
lengthways into 3 mm/⅛ in slices
60 g/2 oz butter
170 g/6 oz Gruyère cheese,
grated
60 g/2 oz Parmesan cheese,
grated
150 ml/¼ pint double cream
salt and freshly ground black
pepper

1. If you slice the potatoes ahead of time, rinse, pat dry with kitchen paper towels and keep in a damp tea cloth to prevent discolouring.
2. Preheat the oven to 180°C/350°F/Gas 4. Generously butter the base of an ovenproof dish, then arrange a layer of about a third of the potato slices, overlapping, over the bottom. Sprinkle over about one-third of each of the cheeses and pour over about a third of the cream. Cut the remaining butter into small dice and sprinkle about a third over the top; season to taste with salt and pepper.
3. Make two further layers in the same way. Cover with foil and cook in the oven for 1¼–1½ hours or until the potatoes are tender. Test for doneness with a sharp knife.
4. Remove the foil about 15 minutes before the end of cooking time to brown the top of the potatoes.

UNCOOKED DISHES

Cucumber and chive mousse

Serves 4

1 medium cucumber
150 g/5 oz cottage cheese
85 ml/3 fl oz thick mayonnaise
1 heaped tsp caster sugar
2 pinches of salt
freshly ground black pepper
½ sachet powdered gelatine
2 tsp finely chopped chives
85 ml/3 fl oz whipping cream
chopped parsley

1. Peel the cucumber, quarter it length-ways, remove the seeds and chop the flesh very, very finely.
2. Rub the cottage cheese through a fine sieve into a bowl. Stir in the mayonnaise to make a smooth mixture.
3. Put the water into a saucepan. Stir in the sugar, salt and a little pepper. Sprinkle the gelatine over the top, stir and allow to rest for a few minutes. Then put the pan over low heat and stir to dissolve. Set the pan aside to cool. When the gelatine mixture is cool stir it into the cottage cheese mixture. Mix in the cucumber and chives.
4. Beat the cream until stiff and fold it in. Spoon the mixture into 4 × 7.5 cm/3 inch ramekin dishes. Cover and put the ramekins into the refrigerator to chill until set.
5. To serve, run a knife round the inside of the ramekin to loosen the mousse. Put the ramekin upside down on to a serving plate and give it a sharp tap to unmould the mousse. Garnish with chopped parsley.

Celeriac rémoulade

Celeriac rémoulade

Serves 4

4 lettuce leaves
salt and freshly ground black pepper
225 g/8 oz celeriac, peeled and coarsely
grated
½ small onion, finely chopped
225 ml/8 fl oz thick mayonnaise
2 tsp lemon juice
1 tbsp French mustard
1 tbsp chopped chives

1. Place a lettuce leaf on each plate and sprinkle with salt and pepper to taste.
2. Combine the remaining ingredients together in a mixing bowl, ensuring that the celeriac is well coated with the mayonnaise. Season to taste. Spoon on to the lettuce and sprinkle with the chives.
3. Serve as an appetizer.

Taramasalata

Serves 4

120 g/4 oz fresh white breadcrumbs
5 tbsp olive oil
120 g/4 oz smoked cod's roe, skinned
juice of 1 lemon
1 clove garlic, crushed

1. Put the breadcrumbs into a blender with 1 tbsp of oil and blend until smooth. Add alternately, 1 tbsp cod's roe and 1 tbsp oil, until both ingredients are used up. Add the lemon juice and garlic and purée briefly until a smooth thick paste is formed.
2. Season with black pepper and spoon into individual ramekins or pots.

Aïoli sauce (with crudités)

This is garlic mayonnaise, one of the oldest sauces in the Mediterranean area. It is served here with crudités – raw vegetables – but goes equally well with fish, rabbit and cold meat dishes. For best results, make aïoli about 8 hours ahead of serving time to allow the garlic to flavour the mayonnaise. You can use the left over egg whites to make meringues, or for Pear and rum meringue (see page 76).

Serves 6 as a dipping sauce

2 egg yolks
225 ml/8 fl oz olive oil
5 large cloves garlic
pinch of sea salt (optional)
salt and freshly ground pepper
1 tbsp lemon juice
a selection of raw vegetable pieces (see below)

1. In a small bowl, beat the egg yolks until they are pale, then add the oil very slowly, a little at a time, beating vigorously as you go.
2. Purée the garlic in a mortar with a little oil and adding just a pinch of sea salt, if liked.
3. Adjust the seasoning and stir in the lemon juice. Mix well. Stir the garlic purée mixture into the mayonnaise and set aside to allow the flavour to develop.
4. Serve as a delicious appetizer with sliced green and red peppers, carrot, celery and fennel slices, radishes and cauliflower florets.

Pesto sauce

This is one of the most famous sauces in Italy and must be made with fresh basil if at all possible – dried basil will not do. Serve with fresh pasta if this is obtainable. Pesto sauce has a problem in that it discolours if not used immediately, so it is best either to serve it at once or bottle it in a screw-top jar with a film of olive oil on top and refrigerate until needed.

Serves 4

60 g/2 oz basil leaves
2 cloves garlic
60 g/2 oz pine nuts
1 tbsp melted butter
2 tbsp grated Parmesan cheese
4 tbsp olive oil
1 tbsp grated Pecorino or Romano cheese
salt and freshly ground black pepper

1. Put all the ingredients into a blender and mix at a high speed for 45 seconds. If the sauce is too thick add a tablespoon or two of water.
2. Scrape the mixture out of the blender and serve with cooked pasta such as noodles or thin spaghetti. A crisp dry white wine, such as an Italian Frascati, would be an excellent accompaniment.

Avocado guacamole

Serves 4

2 ripe avocados, peeled and stoned
1 tbsp finely chopped onion
2 cloves garlic, crushed
1 tbsp olive oil
1 tbsp lemon juice
salt
Tabasco sauce to taste

1. Sprinkle the avocados with lemon juice as you prepare them to avoid discolouring. Mash the avocado flesh with the onion and garlic until smooth.
2. Beat in the olive oil, lemon juice and salt to taste, then add Tabasco until the guacamole reaches the required degree of hotness.
3. Chill in the refrigerator for at least 30 minutes. Serve as an appetizer with tacos or tortillas, or with sliced raw vegetables.

Greek avocado

Serves 4

2 avocados, halved and stoned
340 g/12 oz feta cheese, diced
6 tbsp olive oil
2 tbsp white wine vinegar
salt and freshly ground pepper
2 tsp dried oregano

1. Arrange the avocado halves on individual serving plates.
2. Combine the remaining ingredients, except the oregano, in a mixing bowl. Spoon about a quarter of the mixture into each of the avocado cavities and sprinkle the oregano over the tops.
3. Serve immediately, as an appetizer; or, to serve 2, with salad, as a light lunch.

Avocado with orange cottage cheese

Serves 4

2 medium oranges
225 g/8 oz thick cottage cheese
freshly ground black pepper
12 walnut halves, chopped
2 avocados

1. Using a potato peeler, remove a few thin strips of orange peel. Cut the peel into very thin, small matchstick pieces. Squeeze the juice from one of the oranges and set aside.
2. In a medium-sized bowl, mix together the cottage cheese, 4 tablespoonfuls of the orange juice and a few grindings of black pepper.
3. Just before serving, cut the avocados in half and remove the stones. Spoon the cottage cheese mixture into the avocado holes and sprinkle the tops decoratively with the reserved orange peel and walnut halves.
4. Serve immediately, as a hearty appetizer. Or it will serve 2, as a light summer snack meal, accompanied by brown bread and butter.

Green eggs

Serves 6

1 packet watercress
1 bunch mixed fresh herbs (parsley,
*   tarragon, chives, chervil and sorrel)*
170 ml/6 fl oz thick mayonnaise
3 tbsp double cream
salt and freshly ground black pepper
6 hard-boiled eggs, shelled

1. Reserve 4 watercress sprigs for the garnish. Remove the stalks from the rest. Chop the watercress leaves and the mixed herbs together very finely.
2. Add the chopped herbs to the mayonnaise with the cream, and salt and pepper to taste.
3. Cut the hard-boiled eggs in half and arrange 2 halves on each plate. Spoon the green mayonnaise over the eggs. Garnish with the reserved watercress and serve as an appetizer.

Dieter's salad

Serves 2

1 × 200 g/7 oz tin tuna fish, drained
2 carrots, grated
1 sweet and sour gherkin, chopped
2 sticks celery, chopped
salt and freshly ground black pepper
pinch of grated nutmeg (optional)
low calorie mayonnaise to bind
340 g/12 oz cottage cheese
2 tsp chopped chives

1. Combine all the ingredients, except the cottage cheese and chives, in a bowl.
2. Arrange half the cottage cheese decoratively on each of 2 individual serving plates then arrange half of the tuna fish mixture around it. Scatter the chives on top just before serving.

Green eggs

Feta cheese salad

Feta cheese salad

Serves 4–6

4 medium tomatoes, quartered
I cucumber, peeled and halved
*   lengthways*
I medium onion, thinly sliced
120 g/4 oz feta cheese, diced
16 black olives, stoned
finely chopped parsley and basil

Dressing

4 tbsp olive oil
2 tbsp lemon juice
I clove garlic, crushed
salt and freshly ground black pepper

1. Put the tomatoes into a bowl. Cut the cucumbers across into 5 mm/¼ inch slices and add to the tomatoes along with the onion, feta cheese and olives.

2. Make the dressing by beating all the ingredients thoroughly together. Pour the dressing over the salad and toss well to mix.

3. Arrange the salad on a serving platter and sprinkle generously with the parsley and basil.

Peach and cottage cheese salad

Many years ago my company, the Express Dairy in London, used to own a very famous chain of restaurants called The Chicken Inns. They are no longer with us today, but were in well-known sites such as Leicester Square, Piccadilly, Oxford Street and Haymarket. This is one of the dishes that I devised for them. Serve as a delicious, light lunch dish.

For each serving
2 crisp lettuce leaves
1 ½ fresh peaches, skinned
4 tbsp cottage cheese
2 tbsp salad cream
6 cucumber slices

1. Arrange the lettuce leaves on a serving plate. Put the peach halves in a straight line on the lettuce, leaving enough room between each one for the cottage cheese.
2. Put 2 tbsp of cottage cheese on either side of the centre peach half. Spoon the salad cream gently across the top of the peaches.
3. Garnish with the cucumber slices to add colour.

Waldorf salad

This salad is traditionally believed to have been invented by a chef at the Waldorf Astoria Hotel in New York during the 1930s. It is very rich, a particularly good complement to cold meat or poultry dishes. The 'correct' liqueur to use has always been a matter for conjecture and debate: orange curaçao is one that particularly lends itself to the other flavours in the recipe.

Cucumber and mint sambal

This is a deliciously refreshing side dish to serve with curry or chilli – or indeed any other hot spicy dish.

Serves 4
1 cucumber, peeled, quartered
  lengthways and seeded
salt
1 green pepper, seeded and cut into
  2.5 cm/1 inch strips
10 spring onions, cut into 2.5 cm/1 inch
  strips
1 tbsp chopped mint
2 tbsp lemon juice
300 ml/½ pint natural yogurt

1. Cut the cucumber into 2.5 cm/1 inch strips. Put them on a teacloth, sprinkle with salt and leave to drain for at least 30 minutes.
2. Put the drained cucumber, green pepper, spring onions and mint into a serving bowl and stir in the lemon juice. Chill in the refrigerator until ready to serve.
3. Just before serving, mix in the yogurt.

Serves 6
2 large red apples, cored and sliced
4 celery stalks, chopped
85 g/3 oz chopped walnuts
120 ml/4 fl oz thick mayonnaise
2 tbsp liqueur (see left)
1 tbsp lemon juice
6 large lettuce leaves

1. Mix together all the ingredients, except the lettuce, in a bowl.
2. Arrange a lettuce leaf on each serving plate and pile the salad on top.

Steak tartare

Serves 2

225 g/8 oz fillet steak, minced
2 egg yolks
1 sweet and sour gherkin, finely
*   chopped*
1 tsp finely chopped onion
1 tsp finely chopped capers
Worcestershire sauce to taste
salt and freshly ground black
*   pepper*
1 tbsp chopped parsley
several dashes of Tabasco
*   sauce*
2 lettuce leaves
4 anchovy fillets (optional)

1. Combine the ingredients, except the
lettuce and anchovy fillets if used, in a
mixing bowl.
2. Form into 2 large patties, each about
10 cm/4 inches in diameter and flatten each
one slightly.
3. Place a lettuce leaf on each of 2 serving
plates and top with the patties. If using the
anchovy fillets, arrange two on top of each
patty. Serve with fresh salad as a light lunch
or supper. A medium dry white wine, or a
soft rosé, would go well with this dish.

Japanese sliced fish

Always use absolutely fresh fish for this
dish: check for firm flesh, clear, bright eyes
if the head is still attached, and no odour.
Octopus (parboiled), squid, abalone, sea
bass, bream, striped bass, prawns and
shrimps are some of the seafoods which can
be prepared in this way. Raw chicken
breasts, sprinkled with lemon juice, can
also be treated in this way.

Serves 4

750 g/1 ½ lb sea bass, tuna or other
*   saltwater fish, filleted*
170 g/6 oz white radish, shredded
1 carrot, shredded
4–5 spring onions, trimmed and
*   shredded*
a few mange-tout peas
a few cooked, unshelled giant
*   prawns*
1 tbsp green horseradish (wasabi)
a few lemon wedges
1 tbsp freshly grated ginger root
light soy sauce to taste

1. Remove any skin, bones and dark sec-
tions from the fish. Cut the fish diagonally
into slices about 2.5 cm/1 inch long and
5 mm/¼ inch thick. Arrange all the fish
slices on a platter with the vegetables and
prawns.
2. Mix the horseradish to a thick paste with
a little water and put on the platter with the
lemon wedges and ginger. Pour soy sauce
into small individual serving bowls.
3. To serve, allow each diner to add horseradish and ginger to his or her soy sauce to
taste. The fish pieces and vegetables are
then dipped lightly into the sauce before
eating.
4. Serve with Japanese-style or plainly
cooked long-grain rice.

DESSERTS AND BAKING

Chocolate profiteroles

Serves 4

70 g/2½ oz plain flour
½ tsp salt
60 g/2 oz unsalted butter
120 ml/4 fl oz water
2 eggs
1 egg beaten with 2 tbsp milk

Filling

chocolate ice cream (see page 79)

Sauce

*225 g/8 oz plain chocolate, broken into
  pieces*
225 ml/8 fl oz water
1 tbsp brandy or rum (optional)
*100 g/3½ oz unsalted butter, cut into
  pieces*

1. Butter a baking sheet and cover with nonstick baking parchment. Preheat the oven to 200°C/400°F/Gas 6.
2. To make the choux pastry, sift the flour and salt on to a sheet of greaseproof paper. Put the butter and water into a saucepan and set over low heat. When the butter has melted, increase the heat and bring to the boil. Remove the pan from the heat and pour in the flour immediately. Beat to mix. Return the pan to moderate heat and stir constantly until the mixture forms a ball that comes away cleanly from the sides of the pan. Remove the pan from the heat and leave to cool for a few minutes.

3. Add the eggs one at a time, beating after each addition. Continue beating until the dough is smooth and shiny.
4. Spoon the dough into a piping bag fitted with 2 cm/¾ inch plain nozzle and pipe 16 walnut-sized balls, 4 cm/1½ inches apart, on to the baking sheet. Brush all over with the egg and milk mixture and bake for 15–20 minutes or until the puffs are firm and golden in colour. A few minutes before they are done, pierce them with a fork to release the steam. Remove from the oven and cool on wire racks.
5. Meanwhile, make the sauce. Put the chocolate, water and the brandy or rum, if you are using it, into a saucepan over low heat. Stir until the chocolate melts and the mixture is smooth. Remove from the heat and stir in the butter, a little at a time, until the sauce is glossy.
6. When the choux puffs are cool, slice them in half crosswise. Working quickly, spoon the chocolate ice cream into the bottom halves and replace the tops. Put the profiteroles in the freezer for 10 minutes to firm the ice cream.
7. Serve in individual bowls with the chocolate sauce poured over the top.

Note: You can substitute other flavours of ice cream for the chocolate used in this particular recipe – or a Crème pâtissière (see page 86). Chopped fresh fruit folded into stiffly whipped double cream is another favourite filling for Profiteroles.

*ABOVE: Chocolate profiteroles; BELOW:
Chiffon pie (see page 74)*

Chiffon pie

Serves 6

225 ml/8 fl oz milk
135 g/4 ½ oz sugar
200 g/7 oz plain chocolate, broken into
    pieces
2 eggs, separated
1 tbsp powdered gelatine
3 tbsp strong black coffee
340 ml/12 fl oz double cream, whipped

Pastry

170 g/6 oz plain flour
pinch of salt
85 g/3 oz butter
1 small egg, lightly beaten
1–2 tbsp iced water

Topping

225 ml/8 fl oz double cream, whipped
grated chocolate

1. First make the pastry. Sift the flour and salt into a mixing bowl. Add the butter and cut it in with a knife. Using your fingertips rub the butter into the flour until the mixture resembles fine breadcrumbs. Mix the egg with 1 tbsp of the iced water and mix into the flour mixture with the knife. When the dough begins to form, pat lightly into a ball. If the mixture is too dry add the rest of the iced water. Cover the dough and chill in the refrigerator for 30 minutes.
2. Preheat the oven to 190°C/375°F/Gas 5. Roll out the dough on a lightly floured surface to 3–5mm/⅛–¼ inches thick and use to line a greased 23 cm/9 inch fluted deep flan dish. Prick the bottom with a fork, line with foil or greaseproof paper and weigh down with rice or dried beans. Bake in the oven for 15 minutes. Remove the foil and beans and bake for a further 15 minutes or until the pastry is crisp. Cool in the dish before removing the pastry case.

3. To make the filling, combine the milk, 85 g/3 oz of the sugar and the chocolate pieces in a saucepan. Cook over moderate heat, stirring constantly, until the chocolate has melted and the sugar dissolved. Remove from the heat and leave to cool for a few minutes, then whisk in the egg yolks.
4. Dissolve the gelatine in the coffee over low heat and stir into the chocolate mixture. Chill until the mixture begins to set.
5. Whisk the egg whites with the remaining sugar until stiff. Fold the cream and then the egg whites into the chocolate mixture. Pour into the pie shell. Chill in the refrigerator until set.
6. Decorate with the whipped cream and grated chocolate before serving.

Exotic fruit salad

Serves 4–6

1 fresh mango
1 medium pineapple
2 nectarines, peeled and sliced
2–3 kiwi fruit, peeled and each one cut
    into 6 slices
170–225 ml/6–8 fl oz orange juice
120 ml/4 fl oz orange Curaçao
1 banana

1. Peel the mango, then cut the flesh away from the stone. Cut into slices. Prepare the pineapple by topping and tailing, then cutting away the skin. Cut lengthways into 4, and cut away the hard centre. Slice.
2. Put all the fruit, except the kiwi fruit, in a glass dessert bowl. Arrange some of the kiwi slices around the sides.
3. Pour over the orange juice and liqueur, then decorate the centre with remaining kiwi slices. Cover and chill until ready to serve. Just before serving, peel and slice the banana and add to the dish.

Lemon flan

Serves 4–6

150 g/5 oz digestive biscuits, finely crushed
85 g/3 oz ginger biscuits, finely crushed
120 g/4 oz butter, melted
3 tbsp hot water
1 tsp powdered gelatine
grated rind of 1 and juice of 2 lemons
85 g/3 oz caster sugar
2 eggs, separated
225 ml/8 fl oz whipping cream
extra lemon rind
extra whipping cream, stiffly beaten

1. Put the finely crushed biscuits into a bowl. Pour in the melted butter and mix well. Spoon the mixture into a deep flan tin, 25 cm/10 inches in diameter, with a removable bottom. Press and mould the mixture so that it lines the base and sides of the tin. Set aside in the refrigerator while you make the filling.
2. Put the hot water into a cup. Sprinkle the gelatine over the top and stir until it dissolves.
3. Put the grated lemon rind and juice into a large mixing bowl. Add the sugar and egg yolks and beat well. Add the cream slowly and beat well for several minutes or until the mixture is thick and creamy. Beat in the gelatine and put the bowl into the refrigerator.
4. When the lemon mixture has become cold and has begun to set, whisk the egg whites until stiff. Fold the egg whites into the lemon mixture, then pour into the flan case. Return the flan case to the refrigerator and chill for several hours, or until completely set. Remove the flan from the tin case, using the back of a large metal spoon to slide it off the tin bottom. Decorate the filling with extra lemon rind and whipped cream whirls before serving.

Three-fruit summer pudding

Serves 4–6

450 g/1 lb raspberries
225 g/8 oz redcurrants
225 g/8 oz blackberries
225 g/8 oz caster sugar
6 tbsp boiling water
10–12 slices of bread

1. Grease a 1 litre/1¾ pint pudding basin with butter.
2. Using a fork, strip the redcurrants from their stalks. Rinse under cold water, drain and mix with the raspberries. Hull the blackberries, if necessary, and add to the bowl.
3. Put the sugar and water into a saucepan and heat, stirring until the sugar has dissolved. Add the fruit to the pan and bring just to the boil. Remove from the heat immediately and allow to stand for 2 minutes.
4. Cut the crusts from the bread and line the pudding basin with several slices, making sure that they fit together neatly. Spoon the fruit filling into the basin then cover with the remaining bread slices.
5. Cover the pudding with a plate with a weight on top (a large full tin will do). Place in the refrigerator overnight.
6. To turn out the pudding on to the plate, first remove the weight from the plate, then grasp the plate and basin together and reverse, giving the basin a good sharp shake. The pudding should slide out very easily.

Pear and rum meringue

This very special, delicious dessert is surprisingly easy to make and provides an excellent way to use up any leftover egg whites. It can be served warm or cold.

Serves 6–8

3 tbsp water
30 g/1 oz butter
120 g/4 oz soft brown sugar
1 tsp ground cinnamon
1 kg/2 lb pears
4 trifle sponge cakes, cut in half
30 ratafia biscuits
4–5 egg whites
120 g/4 oz granulated sugar
120 g/4 oz caster sugar
4–5 tbsp white rum

1. Put the water, butter, brown sugar and cinnamon into a large saucepan with the pears. Simmer until the pears are soft (about 10–15 minutes), stirring from time to time. Remove from the heat and cool.

2. When the mixture has cooled, remove the pears and peel and quarter them. Remove the seeds then slice the flesh.

3. Line the sides of a 25 cm/10 inch ovenproof quiche or flan dish with sponge cake halves to cover them completely. Arrange the ratafia biscuits in the centre of the dish.

4. Whisk the egg whites until stiff. Fold in the granulated sugar then beat again until very stiff. Finally, gently and carefully fold in the caster sugar.

LEFT: Strawberry syllabub (see page 78); RIGHT: Pear and rum meringue

5. Moisten the sponge cakes and ratafias with the rum, then spoon the pears into the centre of the dish, to cover the ratafias. Top with the meringue mixture, shaping it into decorative mounds with a large spoon or fork.

6. Put the dish into the oven preheated to 190°C/375°F/Gas 5 and bake for 10–15 minutes or until the decorative tops of the meringue are lightly browned.

Note: Sliced peaches and kirsch can be substituted for the pears and rum.

Strawberry syllabub

Serves 4

120 g/4 oz fresh strawberries
60 g/2 oz caster sugar
430 ml/¾ pint whipping cream
4 tbsp strawberry jelly
1 tbsp water
8 walnut, halves (optional)

1. Reserve 4 strawberries for decoration. Hull and chop the remainder very finely.
2. Whisk the sugar and cream together until stiff. Gently fold in the chopped strawberries until well mixed. Pipe this mixture like a nest, into 4 ramekins or glass dishes.
3. Make a glaze by heating the strawberry jelly gently with the water until melted. Remove from the heat. Dip the reserved whole strawberries into the jelly to glaze and arrange them decoratively on each dish. If desired, arrange 2 walnut halves on each dish.
4. Chill in the refrigerator until ready to serve.

Bitter chocolate ice

Serves 8

600 ml/1 pint milk
150 g/5 oz caster sugar
120 g/4 oz plain chocolate, broken into pieces
85 g/3 oz cocoa powder
285 ml/½ pint double or whipping cream, whipped

1. Put the milk and sugar into a saucepan. Heat gently, stirring until the sugar is dissolved. Bring just to the boil and add the chocolate pieces. Stir until the chocolate melts and the mixture is smooth. Mix in the cocoa powder and, when thoroughly blended, strain into a bowl and leave to cool, stirring occasionally.
2. Fold in the whipped cream. Pour the mixture into a churn or into ice trays. If using a churn, follow the manufacturer's instructions. If using ice trays, after freezing for 30 minutes, stir the frozen edges of the mixture into the centre breaking up any large crystals as you do so. Repeat this every hour until the ice is thick and smooth, then freeze until ready to serve.

Chocolate roulade

Serves 6

85 g/3 oz plain cooking chocolate, broken into pieces
3 eggs, separated
285 ml/½ pint whipping cream
85 g/3 oz caster sugar
icing sugar

1. Preheat the oven to 180°C/350°F/Gas 4. Grease a 45 × 30 cm/18 × 12 inch baking sheet. Line it with greaseproof paper and grease the paper.
2. Melt the chocolate in a double saucepan.
3. Beat the egg yolks. In a separate bowl, whisk the egg whites until stiff. Mix the melted chocolate into the egg yolks, then fold the egg whites into the mixture.
4. Pour on to the prepared baking sheet and bake for 20 minutes. Remove the baking sheet from the oven and leave to cool.
5. Turn the sponge out upside down on to a fresh piece of greaseproof paper and leave overnight.
6. Next day, beat the cream and caster sugar until thick and spread evenly over the sponge. Carefully roll up the roulade as you would a Swiss roll.
7. Dust with icing sugar and serve.

Laws chocolate mousse

You can either serve this mousse in one large glass bowl or, better still, use 6 large wine glasses and top each one with a little whipped cream and extra dessert chocolate, grated or made into curls.

Serves 6

340 g/12 oz cooking chocolate, broken into pieces
30 g/1 oz butter
60 g/2 oz caster sugar
2 tbsp water
6 eggs, separated
1 × 285 g/10 oz tin sterilized cream

1. Put the chocolate into a heatproof bowl along with the butter, sugar and water. Set over a pan of barely simmering water and heat gently until the mixture is melted and smooth, stirring frequently. Remove from the heat.
2. Beat the egg yolks until just mixed. In a separate bowl, whisk the egg whites until stiff.
3. Beat the egg yolks into the chocolate mixture, then fold in the cream.
4. Finally, fold in the beaten egg whites and spoon into the chosen serving dish or dishes.
5. Serve well chilled.

Chocolate ice cream

Serves 6–8

120 g/4 oz plain chocolate, broken into pieces
600 ml/1 pint milk
7 egg yolks
120 g/4 oz caster sugar

1. Put the chocolate in a saucepan. Add just enough milk to cover the bottom of the pan and place over low heat. Stir continuously until the mixture forms a smooth paste, then gradually stir in the rest of the milk. Remove from the heat.
2. In a mixing bowl, whisk the egg yolks with the sugar until the mixture falls off the whisk in a thick ribbon. Gradually whisk in the chocolate flavoured milk.
3. Pour the custard back into the saucepan and return to a medium heat. Stir until the custard thickens and coats the back of a spoon but do not let it boil. Strain into a bowl and cool in the refrigerator or over ice cubes.
4. Pour the custard into a churn or into ice trays. If using a churn, follow the manufacturer's instructions. If using ice trays, freeze for 30 minutes or until the ice cream begins to set around the edges. Turn into a mixing bowl and whisk until smooth. Return to the trays and freeze for another 30 minutes.
5. Repeat whisking and freezing at 30 minute intervals until the ice cream is thick and smooth.
6. Freeze until ready to serve.

Applescotch

Serves 6

450 g/1 lb cooking apples, peeled, cored
and chopped
60 g/2 oz butter
grated rind and juice of 1 lemon
3 eggs, separated
6 tbsp whisky
285 ml/½ pint double or whipping cream
170 g/6 oz caster sugar
6 even-sized, large red dessert apples
marzipan or chocolate leaves, to decorate
(see recipe)

1. Put the cooking apples into a saucepan with the butter and lemon rind. Cover and cook gently for 20 minutes or until tender. Beat to a pulp and stir in the egg yolks. Continue cooking very gently until the mixture thickens. Beat in the whisky and set aside to cool.

2. Whip the cream until thick and fold into the apple purée together with half of the sugar. Put the mixture into a freezer container, cover and freeze for 1–1½ hours or until ice crystals have formed around the edge. Tip the mixture into a large mixing bowl.

3. Whisk the egg whites until stiff and then whisk in the remaining sugar. Fold lightly but evenly into the apple mixture. Return to the freezer while you prepare the 'apple cases'.

4. Cut a thin slice from the stalk end of each apple and set aside. Carefully hollow out the apples removing the core and some of the flesh to leave a shell about 1.5 cm/½ inch thick. Brush all the exposed surfaces of the apples with the lemon juice, including the lids.

5. Remove the apple ice cream from the freezer, spoon some into the hollowed out apples and cover with the lids. Wrap each apple in freezer wrap and return to the freezer until needed. Remove the apples from the freezer 30 minutes before serving, to soften slightly.

6. To make the decoration, cut leaf shapes from thinly rolled green tinted marzipan, or, alternatively, lightly oil bay leaves and coat one side with melted chocolate. Leave to set. Once the chocolate is hard it will peel away neatly from the bay leaf.

7. Serve each apple with an accompanying leaf.

Baked banana crunch

Serves 2

30 g/1 oz butter
2 firm bananas
1 tbsp brown sugar
1 tbsp Coco-ribe liqueur
1 tbsp Crunch Nut Topping

1. Preheat the oven to 160°C/300°F/Gas 2. Grease the bottom of a shallow baking dish with a little of the butter.

2. Peel the bananas and cut them in half. Slice each half into 3 on the diagonal. Put the bananas into the baking dish.

3. Melt the remaining butter and spoon over the bananas, then spoon the sugar and liqueur over the top. Put the dish into the oven and bake for 20–25 minutes or until brown and bubbling.

4. Remove the dish from the oven, sprinkle the Crunch Nut Topping over the bananas and serve.

Applescotch

Elderflower sorbet

If you are in the countryside when the elder bushes and trees are in bloom, it is well worth collecting a carrier bag or two of the flowers – they make delightful fritters and sorbets.

Serves 6

24 elderflower heads
1.5 litres/2¼ pints water
550 g/18 oz caster sugar
juice of 3 lemons
2 egg whites

1. Wash the elderflowers thoroughly and pat dry with paper towels.
2. Bring the water to the boil in a large saucepan, then add the sugar. Reduce the heat and stir until the sugar dissolves. Remove the pan from the heat, add the flowers to the syrup and steep for 30 minutes.
3. Strain the mixture into a bowl, stir in the lemon juice and set aside to allow to cool completely.
4. Pour into freezer trays and freeze for about 1 hour or until it is tacky. Remove from the freezer and turn out into a mixing bowl.
5. Whisk the egg whites until they are stiff and fold into the elderflower mixture. Return to the freezer trays and freeze until solid.
6. Remove from the freezer about 15 minutes before serving to allow to soften slightly.

Crème brûlée

This is a lovely soft custard covered with burnt sugar. It is easy to make yet difficult to achieve perfection. The custard can very easily curdle if you do not keep your eye on it.

Serves 6

7 egg yolks
225 g/8 oz caster sugar
1 tsp vanilla essence
825 ml/1½ pints whipping cream
demerara sugar

1. Beat the egg yolks lightly with the sugar and vanilla.
2. Put the cream into the top half of a double boiler. Fill the bottom pan half full of water and bring it to barely simmering point.
3. Put the top pan in position and, using a wooden spoon, slowly stir the egg yolk mixture into the cream. Continue stirring gently until the custard thickens enough to coat the back of the spoon reasonably thickly.
4. Remove the pan from the heat and pour the custard through a strainer into a flameproof bowl, or, if you prefer, into individual ramekin dishes. (I think a bowl is better because the sugar topping seems to cook better that way.) Chill the bowl or dishes in the refrigerator for 4 hours.
5. Preheat the grill to hot. Put the bowl or dishes with the custard into a larger bowl filled with ice cubes. Sprinkle the top of the custard evenly with 2 or 3 tbsp of demerara sugar and place it under the grill. When the sugar has melted and browned (be careful not to burn it), remove and cool the custard for 2 hours. The sugar should harden on top like thin caramel toffee. Serve with cold runny cream.

Lemon cream

Serves 4

12 ratafia biscuits
1 tbsp flaked almonds, toasted
85 ml/3 fl oz gin
285 ml/½ pint whipping or double
  cream
½ tbsp icing sugar
rind and juice of 1 lemon
1 egg white, stiffly beaten

1. Put 3 ratafias into each of 4 dessert glasses. Sprinkle over a few flaked almonds and about 1 tsp of gin.
2. Beat the cream and icing sugar together until stiff. Fold in the lemon rind and juice, then slowly beat in the remaining gin. Fold in the beaten egg white.
3. Spoon the cream into the dessert glasses and chill until ready to serve.

Apple bake

Serves 4–6

225 g/8 oz plain flour,
  sifted
½ tsp salt
2 tbsp brown sugar
120 g/4 oz margarine, cut into
  pieces
1 egg, beaten
60 ml/2 fl oz sour cream
450 g/1 lb cooking apples, peeled,
  cored and finely chopped
120 g/4 oz white sugar
1 tbsp cornflour
¼ tsp ground cinnamon
2 digestive biscuits,
  crumbled
1 tbsp milk

1. Combine the flour, salt and brown sugar together in a mixing bowl. Add the margarine and cut it into the flour mixture with a knife until the mixture resembles fine breadcrumbs. Beat in the egg, then the sour cream and mix to a firm dough. Cover and chill in the refrigerator for 30 minutes.
2. Preheat the oven to 230°C/450°F/Gas 8. Mix the chopped apples, white sugar, cornflour and cinnamon together until well blended.
3. Divide the dough in half. Roll out one half on a lightly floured board to a 3 mm/⅛ inch thick round. Lift the round on to an oiled baking sheet and sprinkle with the crumbled biscuits. Discard any excess juice from the apple mixture then spread it over the top of the dough, to within about 1.5 cm/½ inch of the edges. Brush the edges with some of the milk.
4. Roll out the remaining dough in the same way, and to the same size. Carefully lay this round over the filling, overlapping the edges. Pinch the two rounds together to enclose the filling completely. Prick the top with a fork and brush all over with the remaining milk.
5. Bake in the oven for 15 minutes, then reduce the heat to 180°C/350°F/Gas 4 and cook for 20 minutes or until the pastry is brown and crisp.
6. Serve hot as a dessert with custard or whipped cream or allow to cool and serve, in wedges, as a cake.

Chocolate whisky malakoff

Serves 6-8

18 sponge finger biscuits
120 g/4 oz butter
120 g/4 oz caster sugar
3 eggs, separated
120 g/4 oz plain chocolate, broken into pieces
2 tbsp whisky
8 tbsp water
dash of Angostura bitters
2 tbsp powdered gelatine
285 ml/½ pint double cream, whipped
grated plain chocolate

1. Lightly oil a 15 cm/6 inch charlotte mould. Trace the base and top of the mould and cut out 2 rounds of greaseproof paper to fit. Put the smaller one in the bottom of the mould and oil it. Line the sides of the mould with sponge finger biscuits, with the rounded, sugary sides facing the sides of the mould. Set aside.

2. In a mixing bowl, cream the butter and sugar until light. Beat in the egg yolks at one at a time. Continue beating until the mixture is pale and thick.

3. In a heatproof bowl placed in a pan of barely simmering water, gently melt the chocolate in 2 tbsp of water and stir into the egg yolk mixture. Mix in the whisky and bitters.

4. In a cup placed in a pan of gently simmering water, dissolve the gelatine in the remaining water. Stir into the egg yolk mixture and allow to cool until on the point of setting.

5. Whisk the egg whites until stiff and fold into the mixture. Pour the mixture into the mould and smooth the top with a knife. Oil the second round of greaseproof paper and place it on top. Put in the refrigerator to set for 4-6 hours.

6. To serve, turn out the malakoff on to a serving plate. Remove the greaseproof paper and pipe florets of whipped cream around the top and base and sprinkle with grated chocolate.

LEFT: Chocolate whisky malakoff; RIGHT: Chocolate caraque gateau (page 86)

Sponge finger biscuits

Makes 18 biscuits

3 eggs, separated
85 g/3 oz caster sugar
100 g/3½ oz plain flour, sifted
icing sugar, sifted

1. Line baking sheets with nonstick baking parchment. Preheat the oven to 180°C/ 350°F/Gas 4. Cream the egg yolks and sugar together until thick and pale.

2. In another bowl, whisk the egg whites until stiff and fold them into the creamed mixture together with the flour.

3. Put the mixture into a piping bag fitted with a plain 1 cm/½ inch nozzle. Pipe finger lengths of the mixture on to the lined baking sheets. Dust the biscuits with the icing sugar and bake for 10–12 minutes or until golden. Cool on a wire rack.

Strawberry tart

Pâte sucrée is a sweet short crust pastry with which the French make those incredibly delicious fruit tarts. You can use almost any fruit in season, provided that it is not too juicy. You can also use frozen blackcurrants as they hold so well. If you use apples, slice and arrange in overlapping layers and bake for an extra 10–15 minutes, but reduce the baking blind of the pastry to 15 minutes.

Serves 4–6

750 g/1 ½ lb strawberries, washed
red quick-set jelly glaze

Pâte sucrée

120 g/4 oz plain flour
pinch of salt
60 g/2 oz unsalted butter, softened
60 g/2 oz caster sugar
2 egg yolks

Crème pâtissière

2 tsp plain flour
2 tsp cornflour
2 tbsp caster sugar
1 egg
285 ml/½ pint milk
15 g/½ oz butter

1. First make the pastry. Sift the flour and salt on to your work surface. Make a well in the centre and put in the butter, sugar and egg yolks. Using fingertips, mix the butter, sugar and egg yolks together, gradually drawing in the flour. When all the flour is incorporated lightly knead the dough until smooth. Pat the dough into a ball, cover and refrigerate for 1 hour.
2. Preheat the oven to 220°C/425°F/Gas 7. Roll out the pastry on a floured board. Lift it on to a 20 cm/8 inch tart tin and press it neatly into the tin. Trim edges. Line the

pastry with foil or greaseproof paper and weigh down with dried beans or rice. Put the tart tin in the oven and bake for 15 minutes. Remove the foil and beans and continue baking for a further 5 minutes to brown slightly. Set the pastry case aside to cool.
3. Next make the crème pâtissière. In a mixing bowl, mix the flour, cornflour, sugar and egg with a little milk. In a saucepan, bring the rest of the milk to just under boiling point and pour over the flour mixture, stirring. Pour back into the saucepan and bring to just under boiling point again stirring all the time. Remove the pan from the heat, pour the mixture into the bowl and stir in the butter. Set aside and leave to cool.
4. To assemble the tart, slice a few strawberries in half so that they can fill the holes in between the whole strawberries. Spread the crème pâtissière evenly in the pastry case. Press the strawberries into the cream so that they stand upright. Make up the glaze following the packet instructions, then brush over the strawberries.

Chocolate caraque gâteau

Serves 6–8

4 eggs
120 g/4 oz caster sugar
120 g/4 oz plain flour, sifted
45 g/1 ½ oz butter, melted and cooled

French butter cream

70 g/2 ½ oz caster sugar
150 ml/¼ pint water
2 egg yolks, beaten
150 g/5 oz unsalted butter, softened
120 g/4 oz plain chocolate, melted and
  cooled

Caraque decoration
60 g/2 oz plain chocolate, grated

To finish
30 g/1 oz chocolate, grated
icing sugar

1. Grease an 18 cm/7 inch deep cake tin. Preheat the oven to 180°C/350°F/Gas 4. Put the eggs and sugar into a heatproof bowl and place over a pan of gently simmering water. Whisk until light, creamy and thick enough to hold the impression of the whisk. Remove the bowl from the pan and continue whisking until cool.

2. Fold in the flour and the butter. Pour into the prepared tin and bake for 35–40 minutes or until the cake is firm to the touch and is beginning to shrink from the sides of the tin. Turn the cake out of the tin and cool on a wire rack.

3. To make the butter cream, dissolve the sugar in the water in a small pan. Then boil rapidly until the temperature of the syrup reaches 115°C/240°F or until the syrup forms a firm ball when a small amount is dropped into a cup of cold water. Pour the syrup slowly on to the beaten egg yolks, whisking constantly. When the mixture is cool, thick and fluffy, beat in the butter little by little. Stir in the chocolate and chill the butter cream in the refrigerator.

4. Meanwhile, make the decoration. Melt the chocolate in a bowl placed over hot water, taking care that it does not become too hot and spoil the gloss. Pour the melted chocolate on to a lightly oiled baking sheet and spread thinly with a palette knife. When the chocolate is completely cold, shave it off with a knife to form thin cigarette rolls.

5. To assemble the gâteau, cut the cake in half and sandwich together with half the butter cream. Spread the rest of the butter cream over the top and sides and sprinkle with the grated chocolate. Decorate with caraque rolls and dust with icing sugar.

Cigarettes russes

Cook these biscuits three at a time because speed is required to roll them before they harden.

Makes 10–12 cigarettes
60 g/2 oz butter
2 egg whites
70 g/2½ oz caster sugar
60 g/2 oz plain flour

1. Lightly grease 3 baking sheets. Preheat the oven to 200°C/400°F/Gas 6. Melt the butter in a small saucepan over low heat. Set aside to cool.

2. Whisk the egg whites until frothy. Add the sugar and whisk until stiff.

3. Sift the flour on to the egg whites and fold it in together with the melted butter.

4. Drop teaspoonfuls of the mixture on the baking sheets and spread each one out to form a 7.5 cm/3 inch round. Bake in the oven for 5 minutes or until pale golden in colour.

5. Loosen the biscuits with a palette knife and quickly roll each one around the handle of a wooden spoon. Set the spoons down on a flat surface to prevent the cigarettes unrolling as they cool. Work quickly before they cool and stiffen up.

6. When the cigarettes are firm, remove them from the spoon handles and put them on a wire rack to cool completely before serving.

Brandy chocolate truffles

Serves 4

120 g/4 oz plain chocolate, broken into
    pieces
1 tbsp whipping cream
1 tbsp brandy
120 g/4 oz butter, softened
285 g/10 oz icing sugar, sifted
chocolate vermicelli

1. Put the chocolate pieces in a mixing
bowl. Place the bowl over a pan of hot water
and stir until the chocolate has melted.
Remove the bowl from the pan and mix in
the cream, brandy and butter, stirring until
smooth. Add the sugar and beat to form a
smooth but stiff mixture. Cover and chill in
the refrigerator for several hours until the
mixture firms up.
2. When the mixture is well chilled and
firm, using your hands, form into small
balls and roll in the chocolate vermicelli.

Note: Rum or any liqueur can be substituted for the brandy. And the truffles could
be rolled in grated nuts rather than chocolate vermicelli.

*ABOVE: Brandy chocolate truffles; BELOW:
Florentines*

Florentines

Makes 20–30

170 g/6 oz butter
170 g/6 oz golden syrup
60 g/2 oz plain flour,
    sifted
30 g/1 oz raisins
30 g/1 oz sultanas
85 g/3 oz glacé cherries,
    quartered
120 g/4 oz flaked almonds
170 g/6 oz plain chocolate

1. Grease 3 or 4 baking sheets with lard or
other cooking fat.
2. Melt the butter in a saucepan and pour in
the syrup. Stir in the flour then add the fruit
and almonds. Stir again and remove from
the heat. Set aside and leave the mixture to
cool.
3. Preheat the oven to 190°C/375°F/Gas 5.
Place teaspoonfuls of the mixture on the
prepared baking sheets, spaced well apart –
5–7.5 cm/2–3 inches – as the florentines
will spread while cooking.
4. Bake 2 sheets at a time for 12–16 minutes or until the florentines are golden
brown. Change the position of the baking
sheets halfway through the cooking time to
ensure even cooking.
5. Remove the baking sheets from the oven
and leave to cool on the sheets for a few
minutes. Transfer the florentines to a wire
rack to cool completely.
6. When the florentines are quite cold, melt
the chocolate in a saucepan over low heat.
Spread the undersides of the florentines
with the chocolate. Mark a decorative wavy
pattern with the prongs of a fork and leave
the biscuits face down on the rack to allow
the chocolate to cool and harden. Serve
when cold and set.

Pralines

Pralines are sweetmeats commonly associated with New Orleans and Creole cooking. They are flat, thin and about 7.5–10 cm/3–4 inches in diameter, and break easily when touched.

Traditionally they have a pecan nut in the centre but a walnut half will do if pecans are unobtainable. They keep well if stored in an airtight jar.

Makes 8–12
1 tsp plus extra butter
300 g/11 oz caster sugar
120 ml/4 fl oz whipping cream
½ tsp vanilla essence
12 pecans

1. Before you start, prepare a large sheet of greaseproof paper and butter it generously.
2. Heat the sugar with the cream until the sugar has dissolved. Then boil without stirring until the mixture reaches 120°C/240°F–21°C/250°F. If you do not have a sugar thermometer, drop a little of the mixture into a cup of cold water: it should harden immediately.
3. Beat in the remaining butter and vanilla essence, remove from the heat and set aside to cool slightly. Then beat again until creamy.
4. Drop a level tablespoon at a time onto the buttered paper, spreading the pralines outwards into a circle and leaving some space between each one.
5. Immediately arrange a pecan nut in the centre of each praline before it has time to set.

Banana bread

Makes 1 loaf
100 g/3½ oz margarine
150 g/5 oz brown sugar
2 eggs
285 g/10 oz bananas, peeled and mashed
225 g/8 oz self-raising wholewheat flour (or plain wholewheat flour and 1 tsp baking powder)
½ tsp salt
60 g/2 oz walnuts, chopped

1. Preheat the oven to 180°C/350°F/Gas 4. Grease a 450 g/1 lb loaf tin generously. Cream the margarine and sugar together until light and fluffy. Add the eggs one at a time, and beat until smooth. Blend in the bananas.
2. Mix the flour and salt together, then stir 1 tablespoon into the walnuts to coat. Add the remaining flour to the egg mixture and beat briskly until the batter is smooth and blended.
3. Stir in the walnuts, then turn the mixture into the loaf tin. Bake in the oven for about 1½ hours, or until a skewer inserted into the centre of the bread comes out clean.
4. Remove from the oven and leave in the tin for 5 minutes before transferring the bread to a wire rack to cool.
5. Serve with butter while still slightly warm.

Mincemeat bread

Makes I loaf

120 g/4 oz butter or margarine
85 g/3 oz caster sugar
340 g/12 oz mincemeat
2 eggs
225 g/8 oz self-raising flour

1. Preheat the oven to 180°C/350°F/Gas 4. Grease a 450 g/1 lb loaf tin and dust generously with flour. Cream the butter or margarine and the sugar together until light and fluffy. Add 2 tablespoonfuls of the mincemeat and cream again. Add the eggs to the mixture, one at a time, and beat until smooth.
2. Sift the flour into a bowl then beat 1 tablespoonful into the egg mixture. Gradually add the rest of the flour and mincemeat to the mixture, beating until the batter is smooth.
3. Spoon the batter into the loaf tin and bake in the centre of the oven for about 1 hour, or until a skewer inserted into the centre of the bread comes out clean.
4. Remove from the oven and leave in the tin for 5 minutes before transferring the bread to a wire rack to cool.
5. Serve the bread while still slightly warm.

Rich mince pies

Makes 20

450 g/1 lb mincemeat mixed with 1 ½ tbsp
dark rum

Pastry

285 g/10 oz plain flour
pinch of salt
170 g/6 oz butter
1 egg, lightly beaten
2 tsp water
3 tbsp caster sugar

To finish

1 tbsp milk
1 egg white
1–2 tbsp icing sugar

1. First make the pastry. Sift the flour and salt into a mixing bowl. Dice the butter and then rub it in with your fingertips until the mixture resembles fine breadcrumbs. Add the egg, water and sugar and mix to form a dough. Very lightly firm into a ball, cover and chill in the refrigerator for 15 minutes.
2. Preheat the oven to 200°C/400°F/Gas 6. Grease the tartlet tins. Roll out the dough on a floured surface to 3 mm/⅛ inch thick. Using a 6.25–7.5 cm/2½–3 inch fluted pastry cutter, stamp out 24 dough rounds. Place a dough round in each tartlet tin and, using your thumb and finger, press it up so that it just projects above the top of the tin.
3. Fill each dough-lined tin half full with mincemeat. Brush the top edges of the dough with milk and arrange the remaining rounds on top, sealing together with your fingertips. Make a small cut in the top of each pie to allow steam to escape. Mix the egg white with the remaining milk and brush over the tops of the pies. Put the tins into the oven and bake for 20 minutes.
4. Remove from the oven and cool. Sprinkle with icing sugar before serving.

INDEX

Aioli sauce (with crudités), 66
Apple and cabbage soup, 18
Apple bake, 83
Applescotch, 80, *80*
Artichokes, gratin of, 58
Aubergine and tomato bake,
    53, *53*
Avocado:
    Greek, 67
    guacamole, 67
    with orange cottage cheese,
    67

Beef, 33-6
    braised beef Nivernaise, *32,*
    33
    goulash Galvani, 34
    granny's hamburgers, 33
    grilled sirloin steaks, 34
    olives, *32,* 35
    with pasta, 36
    steak tartare, 71
    vindaloo, 35
Banana bread, 90
Banana crunch, baked, 80
Bisque Creole, 18
Brandy chocolate truffles, *88,*
    89
Brussels sprout purée, 62

Cabbage and apple soup, 18
Cabbage, crispy fried, 62
Calamares a la plancha, 31
Celeriac remoulade, 65, *65*
Cheese:
    avocado with orange
    cottage, 67
    feta cheese salad, 69, *69*
    and peach salad, 70
    sablées, 17, *17*
    stuffed veal and cheese rolls,
    39
Chicken, 46-7
    croquettes with pâté, 22
    fricassee, 46
    with ginger sauce, 47
    liver pâté, easy, 22
    and sweetcorn soup, 19
    Szechuan, 46

tarragon, 47
Chiffon pie, *73,* 74
Chilli dip, 21, *21*
Chocolate:
    bitter chocolate ice, 78
    brandy truffles, *88,* 89
    caraque gâteau, *84,* 86-7
    chiffon pie, 74
    ice cream, 79
    Laws chocolate mousse, 79
    profiteroles, *73, 73*
    roulade, 78
    whisky malakoff, 84, *84*
Cigarettes russes (biscuits), 87
Cod Florentine, 26
Colcannon Galvani, 62
Crab-burgers, 30
Crème brûlée, 82
Cucumber:
    and chive mousse, 65
    and mint sambal, *57,* 70
    sauce, cold, 25, *25*
Cumberland sauce, 44, *44*
Curry, vegetable, 56-7, *57*

Duck, crispy, 48-9, *49*

Eggs:
    green, 68, *68*
    Spanish omelette, 58
Elderflower sorbet, 82

Fennel à la grècque, 20, *21*
Fish and shellfish, 25-31
    Japanese sliced fish, 71
    Madeleine's fish pie, 26
Florentines, *88,* 89
Forest pie, 51
Fruit salad, exotic, 74

Galette potatoes, 63
Gammon with Cumberland
    sauce, 44, *44*
Gardener's broth with sablées,
    17, *17*
Ginger sauce, 47
Goulash Galvani, 34
Gratin dauphinoise, 63
Greek avocado, 67
Green eggs, 68, *68*

Hamburgers, granny's, 33

Hungarian marrow, 59

Ice-cream, chocolate, 79

Japanese sliced fish, 71

Kidneys in mustard, 45, *45*

Lamb:
    korma, 38
    Navarin printanier, 38
    roast leg with herb coating,
    36, *36*
Leeks, shredded, *36,* 62
Lemon cream, 83
Lemon flan, 75
Lemon sole with mustard
    sauce, 27

Madeleine's fish pie, 26
Marrow, Hungarian, 59
Meat balls, creamed, 50
Melon fruit cup, 17
Mincemeat bread, 91
Mince pies, rich, 91
Monkfish, gratin of, 31
Moules à la marinière, 28, *28*
Mushroom sauce, 22, 50
Mushrooms, deep fried with
    chilli dip, 21, *21*
Mustard sauce, 27

Navarin printanier, 38

Onions, stuffed, 61, *61*
Orange cottage cheese with
    avocado, 67
Osso buco, 39

Pancakes:
    with crispy duck, 48-9, *48-9*
    prawn and cheese, 23
Pâté:
    chicken liver, 22
    smoked mackerel, 23
Peach and cottage cheese
    salad, 70
Pear and rum meringue, 76-7,
    77
Pesto sauce, 66
Pizza, 54
Pork, 40-43

cold roast, with prunes and
    pine nuts, 43
fillet sunshine, 42
with orange sauce, 41, *41*
with peppers and ginger, 40,
    41
Pojarsky, 42
Vallée d'Auge, 43
Potatoes:
    galette, 63
    gratin dauphinoise, 63
Pralines, 90
Prawn and cheese pancakes,
    23

Quails' eggs, vol au vents of
    creamed, 59

Rabbit with chestnut purée, 50
Rainbow trout in oatmeal, 27

Sablées, 17, *17*
Salads:
    dieter's, 68
    Feta cheese, 69, *69*
    peach and cottage cheese,
        70
    Waldorf, 70
Salmon with cold cucumber
    sauce, 25, *25*
Sardines with tomato and basil
    sauce, 25
Scallops, vol au vents of, 30
Scampi Galvani, 27
Seafood risotto, 29, *29*
Smoked mackerel pâté, 23
Soups, 17-19
Spanish omelette, 58
Spinach tart, 54-5
Sponge finger biscuits, 85
Steak tartare, 71
Strawberry syllabub, *77*, 78
Strawberry tart, 86
Summer pudding, three-fruit,
    75
Sweetcorn and chicken soup,
    19
Szechuan chicken, 46

Taramasalata, 65
Tomato and aubergine bake,
    53, *53*

Tomato and basil sauce, 25
Tortellini galvani, 53

Veal:
    osso buco, 39
    stuffed veal and cheese rolls,
        39
Vegetable(s), 53-63
    curry, 56-7
    mixed, with cream, 60, *60*
    soup, fresh, 19
Vegetarian rissoles, 55
Vol au vents:
    of creamed quails' eggs, 59
    of scallops and leeks, 30

Waldorf salad, 70
Watercress soup, 19